Houses
DesignSource

Houses
DesignSource

COLLINS DESIGN
An Imprint of HarperCollins Publishers

HOUSES DESIGNSOURCE
Copyright © 2009 COLLINS Design and LOFT Publications

First Edition published in 2009 by:
Collins Design
An Imprint of HarperCollins Publishers
10 East 53rd Street
New York, NY 10022
Tel.: (212) 207-7000
Fax: (212) 207-7654
collinsdesign@harpercollins.com
www.harpercollins.com

Distributed throughout the world by:
HarperCollins Publishers
10 East 53rd Street
New York, NY 10022
Fax: (212) 207-7654

Packaged by
LOFT Publications
Via Laietana, 32 4.° Of. 92
08003 Barcelona, Spain
Tel.: +34 932 688 088
Fax: +34 932 687 073
loft@loftpublications.com
www.loftpublications.com

Editorial coordination
Catherine Collin

Editor and texts:
Aitana Lleonart

Art Director:
Mireia Casanovas Soley

Layout:
Esperanza Escudero
Guillermo Pfaff Puigmartí

Library of Congress Control Number: 2009922099
ISBN: 978-0-06-137470-8

Printed in China

Index

INTRODUCTION

Architecture, like any artistic discipline, is evolving at the same pace as society and is constantly adapting to new trends. Residential architecture is unquestionably one of the architectural typologies offering more creative freedom as it is restricted only by the requirements of owners and the designs of architects. Research on new forms and construction techniques and continual innovations in building materials lead to higher-quality structures that offer greater comfort. Some of these new materials considerably reduce the final cost of construction, meaning the economic factor no longer has a determining role in projects.

Likewise, other aspects dovetail in architectural design, such as climatic and topographical factors, among others.

Dwellings enter into dialog with their environments, or they should. This book therefore includes a chapter on residential property situated in mountainous areas and another on houses built near bodies of water. These locations require a series of solutions to combat, for example, high temperatures, the cold, rain or humidity. Decisions such as the orientation of the dwelling, the distribution of the rooms and the use of insulating materials are critical for achieving better results and greater comfort. The characteristics of the lot must also be taken very much into account, since steep-sloping land often needs a housing project that is stepped on different levels.

This book contains a number of different types of residential projects that are outlined in ten chapters and classified according to the dimensions of the space as well as geographical, constructive and aesthetic criteria. As many of the projects could easily appear in more than one chapter, the salient characteristics of each home were taken into account.

In addition to newly constructed projects, this book has a chapter devoted to home renovation projects. Due to the scarcity of land, especially in big cities, a much more economical alternative is to reform existing buildings instead of demolishing and re-building them. In fact, in some cases, municipal regulations prohibit their demolition. Whatever the reason, the fact is that a high number of renovation and enlargement projects are currently underway. This book contains some examples of these projects, as well as an extensive selection of residential spaces, small houses, minimalist and original designs, spectacular projects, green houses and even prefabricated structures. All these projects offer great ideas and practical solutions.

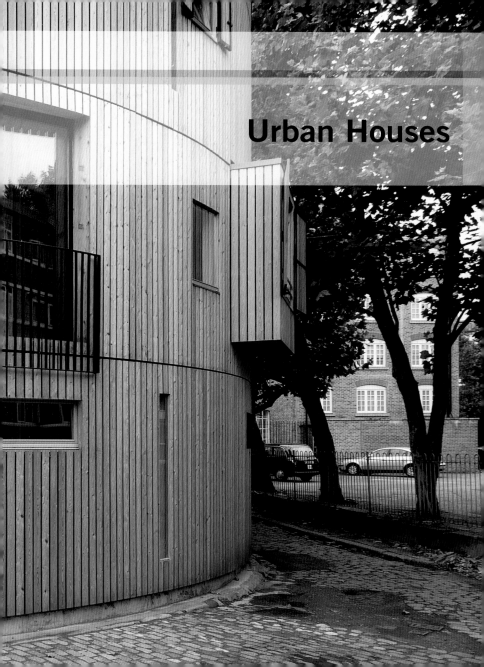

Urban Houses

Didden Village

Architect: MVRDV
Location: Rotterdam, The Netherlands
Photos: © Rob't Hart

This project involved building an extension on the roof of a building. The bedrooms are small separate houses laid out on tiny streets and squares to simulate a city on the rooftop.

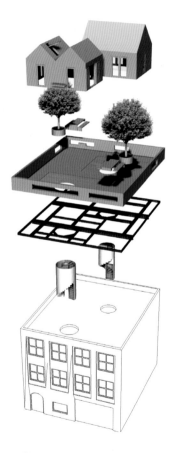

Diagram

19

The use of polyurethane blue in the new extension, which was designed exclusively for this residence, is particularly eye-catching and blends into the sky while contrasting with the warm colors of the interior.

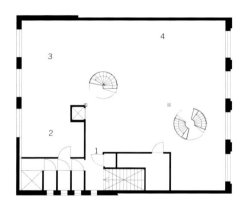

First floor

1. Hall
2. Kitchen
3. Dining room
4. Living room
5. Suite
6. Children's bedroom
7. Terrace

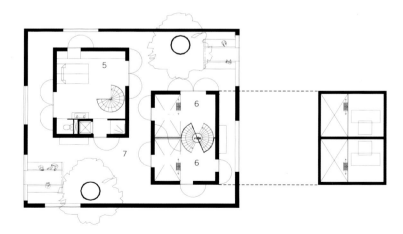

Second floor

The two floors of the house are connected by two spiral staircases, one double and one single. Each provides direct and separate access to one of the three bedrooms.

Each bedroom has been designed as a separate home so that the family members have more privacy. The public areas, i.e., the kitchen, sitting room and dining room, are located on the second floor.

The bedroom/houses have their own private bathrooms. In the main bedroom, the wash basin was installed in the room itself, while the rest of the sanitary ware is surrounded by red walls.

Lagattuta Residence

Architect: SPF:a
Location: Los Angeles, California, USA
Photos: © Claudio Santini

The main door does not lead directly to the house, but to a pathway with a ground glass roof that runs the length of the south façade, past a large patio.

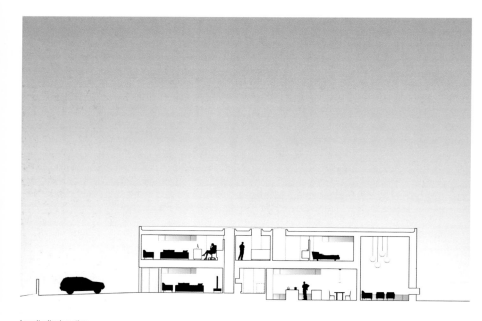

Longitudinal section

The patio is of the same width as the house; the
large exterior is comprised of different areas,
including a garden, lounge and barbeque area.

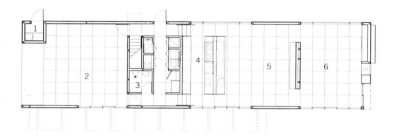

First floor

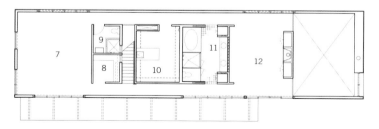

Second floor

1. Storage room
2. Garage
3. Guest bathroom
4. Kitchen
5. Dining room
6. Living room
7. Studio
8. Walk-in closet
9. Guest bathroom
10. Main dressing room
11. Main bathroom
12. Main bedroom

The house is comprised of two floors. The rooms flow freely into one another, as doors and partitions have been kept to a minimum. In addition, the living room has a double-height ceiling.

The public areas are located on the first floor, and the main furniture unit in the kitchen hides a staircase leading to the upper floor, where the main bedroom, two bathrooms and a large studio are located.

House at Montmartre

Architect: Tomoko Anyoji & Yannick Beltrando
Architects
Location: Paris, France
Photos: © Philippe Groscaux

This house is located in the Parisian neighborhood of Montmartre, which has a rich historical heritage and was the cradle of Impressionism. The area underwent extensive development in the late 19th century.

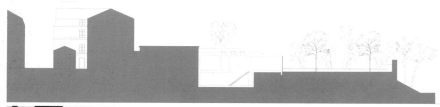

Longitudinal section

Transverse section

The house is divided into two buildings. The main building contains the public areas and the bedroom, while the studio and guest bedroom are located in the adjoining building.

The main and adjoining buildings are partially
buried, which means that the façade is of the same
height as the wall of the neighbor's house, to which
it is attached.

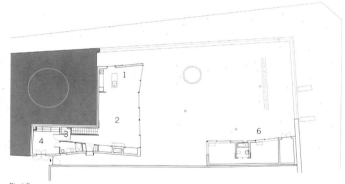

First floor

Basement

1. Kitchen
2. Living/dining room
3. Bathroom
4. Main suite
5. Basement
6. Guest house and studio

The walls facing the garden were replaced with glass and the windows in the bathrooms were covered in iroko panels to ensure privacy.

Helbich House

Architect: SHA Scheffler Helbich Architekten
Location: Dortmund, Germany
Photos: © Christian Eblenkamp

This house was built on a small lot surrounded by hundred-year-old trees. The lower floor is laid out in an open-plan style and the continuity of the space is only broken by a transversely positioned staircase.

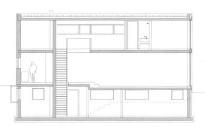

Longitudinal section

Behind the wall of the stairs is the kitchen,
discreetly separated from the rest of the rooms.
To avoid the use of partitions, the first floor
bathroom was built in the adjoining building,
beside the garage.

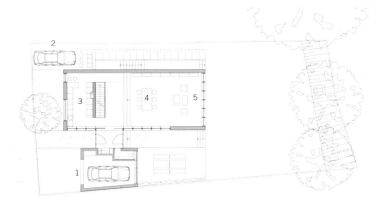

First floor

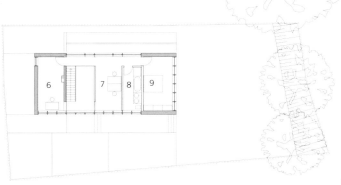

Second floor

1. Indoor garage
2. Outdoor garage
3. Kitchen
4. Dining room
5. Living room
6. Bedroom
7. Studio
8. Bathroom
9. Bedroom

The aluminum frames of the French doors have hinged parts that can be turned to provide shade from the sun or to preserve the privacy of the interior.

The color scheme and materials used in the rest of the house were also used in the bathroom: plaster, slate, wood and glass.

Single Family House

Architect: Aleš Vodopivec
Location: Ljubljana, Slovenia
Photos: © Miran Kambič

Most of the buildings in this area of Ljubljana were constructed in the 18th century. It was therefore decided to carefully reconstruct the façade in keeping with the original buildings.

Transverse section

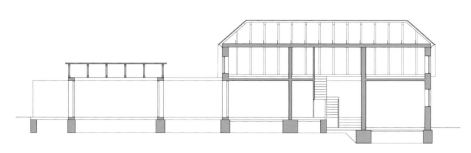

Longitudinal section

Because the owners wanted to live in harmony with nature, spaces such as terraces and a patio were created to provide year-round contact with the exterior.

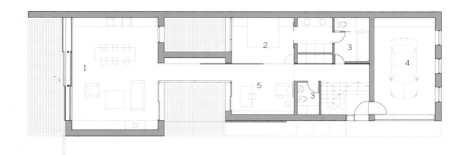

First floor

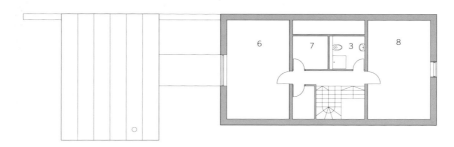

Second floor

1. Living/dining room and kitchen
2. Bedroom
3. Bathroom
4. Garage

5. Library
6. Room
7. Storage space
8. Future kitchen

Sliding panels were installed on the façade overlooking the garden. These blend into the façade and can be opened and closed as needed.

Townhouse in Munich

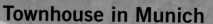

Architect: Landau & Kindelbacher Architekten
Innerarchitekten
Location: Munich, Germany
Photos: © Christian Hacker

This project involved the reconstruction of a villa in the heart of the Schwabing district in Munich. The objectives were clear: to maintain the original structure of the house and to use carefully selected materials and colors.

Front section

The project also had to satisfy the owners' desire
for privacy, despite being located in one of the
city's most central and beautiful streets. Delicate
net curtains were used to protect the interior from
prying eyes while enabling the light to enter.

Basement

First floor

Second floor

Third floor

1. Lounge
2. Sauna
3. Relaxing bathtub
4. Wine cellar
5. Living room
6. Library
7. Kitchen
8. Dining room
9. Main bedroom
10. Bedroom
11. Bathroom
12. Small room
13. Bedroom

The dining room, kitchen, living room and library form a classical sequence that is repeated in most of the houses. Dark wooden floorboards were used in all four rooms to create the feeling of continuity and to contrast with the white stucco ceiling.

A sauna, relaxing bathtub and wine cellar were
installed in the basement of the house to ensure
that the home had an area for relaxation, in
addition to the usual public and private rooms.

Carmarthen Place

Architect: Emma Doherty & Amanda Menage
Location: London, UK
Photos: © Miran Kambič

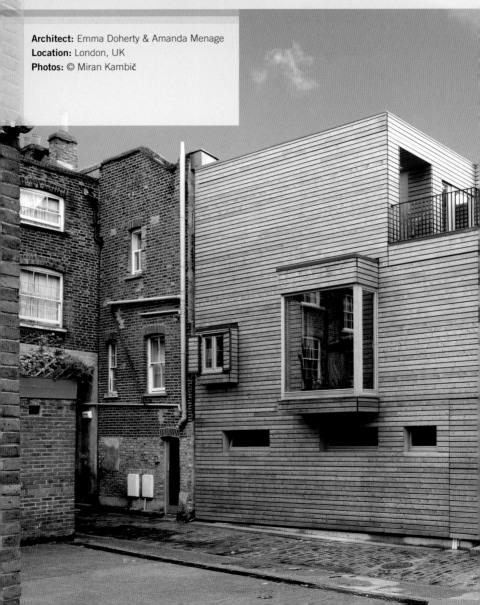

This project involved building an extension to a house in London to create two homes, a studio and an interior patio. It was built on an L-shaped lot that curves slightly at one end.

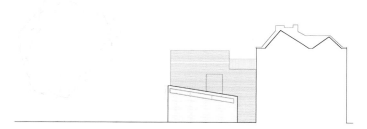

South elevation

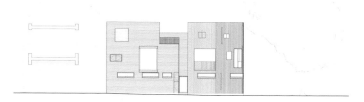

North elevation

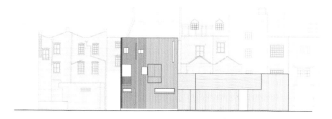

East elevation

After researching the original style of the street where the house is located, the architects decided to use wood in the façade and window shutters in order to maintain its traditional character.

The two buildings are separated by a space that is just one meter wide and three floors high. This serves as a footpath leading to the houses, which have separate entrances.

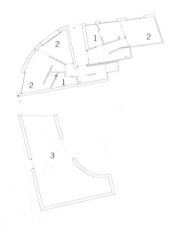

First floor

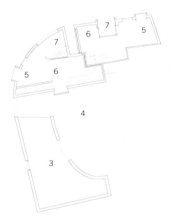

Second floor

Third floor

1. Bathroom
2. Bedroom
3. Studio
4. Patio
5. Dining room
6. Kitchen
7. Interior garden
8. Living room
9. Roof terrace

To enhance privacy, the private areas were located on the first floor and the windows were built high up in the walls. The public areas are on the upper floors.

Architect's Residence

Architect: Nicholas Murray Architects
Location: Melbourne, Australia
Photos: © Shania Shegedyn

The public areas were built on the upper floor to give the occupants a greater feeling of space, more ventilation, and so that they could enjoy the spectacular views.

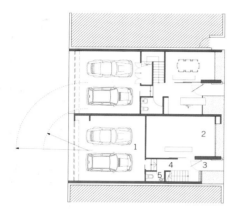

First floor

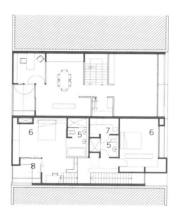

Second floor

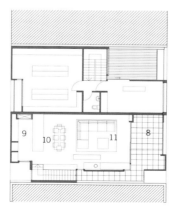

Third floor

1. Garage
2. Office
3. Porch
4. Entrance
5. Bathroom
6. Bedroom
7. Laundry room
8. Terrace
9. Kitchen
10. Dining room
11. Living room

At night, the light from the interior seeps through the wooden slats that form large shutters on the main façade, creating a feeling of warmth and making the house look like a box of light.

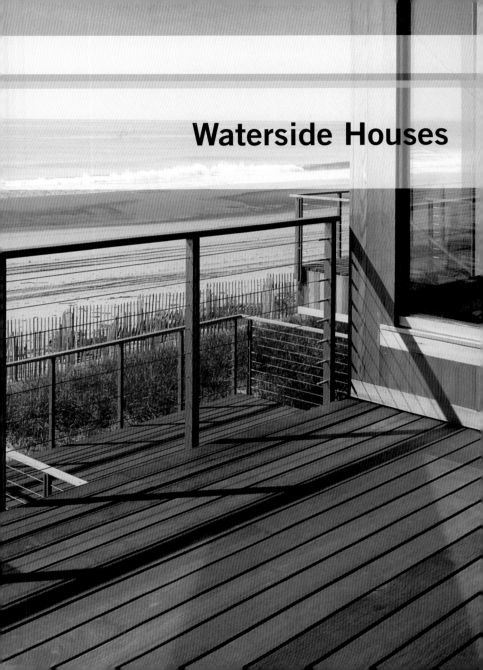

Waterside Houses

Maison Flottante

Architect: Ronan & Erwan Bouroullec
Location: Chatou, France
Photos: © Paul Tahon and Ronan & Erwan Bouroullec

This floating home/studio is moored at Chatou,
the island of the Impressionists, on the River Seine.
The houseboat was designed by the architects
Jean-Marie Finot and Denis Daversin.

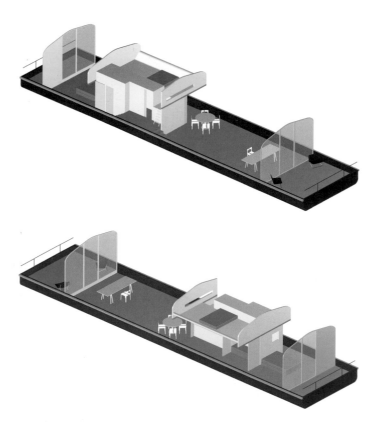

Axonometric plan

An aluminum structure—enclosed in a wooden pergola—denotes the living space which occupies a 16.4 x 75.5 ft. platform. With a total area of 1,184 sq. ft., the living and working areas tend to overlap.

House on Lake Okoboji

Architect: Min | Day
Location: Lake Okoboji, Iowa, USA
Photos: © Larry Gawel

This house sits amid the surrounding trees as if it were a hammock. It is comprised of three connected buildings that open to the exterior as they approach the lake.

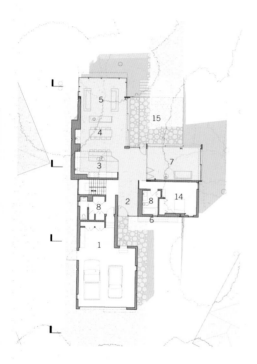

First floor

Second floor

1. Garage/storage space
2. Entrance
3. Kitchen
4. Dining room
5. Living room
6. Skylight
7. Conservatory
8. Bathroom
9. Bedroom with bunk beds
10. Wooden terrace
11. Laundry room
12. Game room
13. Studio
14. Bedroom
15. Terrace

The second floor has irregular shaped windows—
some small and some large—to provide views of
the lake from different angles.

All of the rooms on the upper floor have been painted in vibrant and eye-catching colors. Black is elegantly combined with wood in the bedroom, and red predominates in the bathroom.

House in Buchupuero

Architect: Álvaro Ramírez and Clarisa Elton
Location: Buchupuero, VIII Región del Bío-Bío, Chile
Photos: © Álvaro Ramírez, Clarisa Elton, Carlos Ferrer

Located in a remote area of the central-southern Chilean coast, this house stands on stilts, which reduce the impact of the building on the ground and allow the water to flow freely.

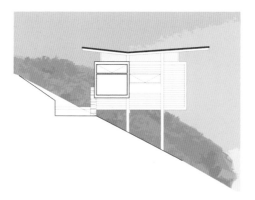

West elevation

1. Interior terrace
2. Living room/kitchen
3. Bedroom
4. Walk-in closet
5. Bathroom

Floor plan

The space is divided into three different areas: the first—with a bedroom and bathroom—is devoted to rest; the second connects the living room and kitchen, and the third—right in the center of the two—is a terrace connecting the two areas.

All rooms have panoramic views of the ocean, thus taking advantage of its privileged location. In addition, the terrace connects the interior with the exterior.

The house is in perfect harmony with the local architecture. Autochthonous materials were used, such as insignis pine and *laja* stone to tile and protect the roof.

Residence Willy & Suzanna Glaesser

Architect: Atelier Oï
Location: Lake Neuchâtel, Switzerland
Photos: © Yves André

When the owners of the house discovered this
marvelous location, they decided to build a home
with a separate section for guests.

Longitudinal section

113

One of the key elements of the project was the color scheme, which they saw as yet another architectural feature. The only condition was to altogether refrain from using the color white.

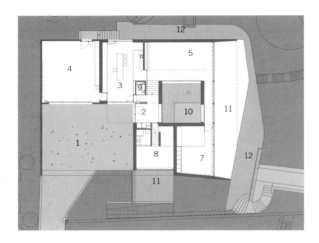

First floor

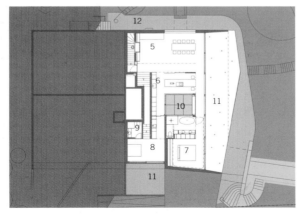

1. Entrance patio
2. Hall
3. Studio
4. Garage
5. Living room
6. Kitchen
7. Bedroom
8. Guest bedroom
9. Bathroom
10. Patio
11. Terrace
12. Garden

Second floor

The house was built on uneven ground and
includes a main building, a patio and two terraces
(one covered and the other exterior).

The predominant colors are yellow, orange and purple. These are alternated in all of the rooms, both interior and exterior, with the darker colors being used in the rooms facing the exterior.

Exploded House

Architect: GAD Architecture
Location: Bodrum, Turkey
Photos: © Ali Bekman, Ozlem Ercil

This house is comprised of three different buildings. Each one was built very close to the other and all three are connected by a glass entrance hall.

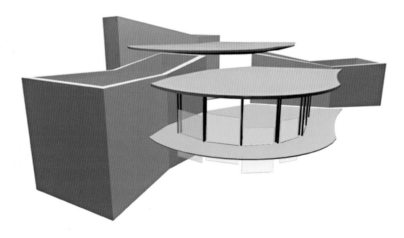

Rendering

The project was designed as a single house and each building serves a specific purpose. Volume A contains the main bedroom and bathroom; building B contains the kitchen and dining room and the third building has a little house for guests and a studio.

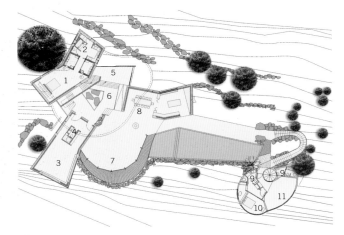

First floor

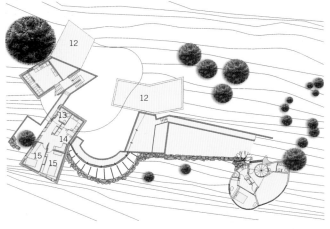

Basement

1. Main bedroom (A)
2. Bathroom (A)
3. Living room (B)
4. Bathroom (B)
5. Entrance
6. Hall
7. Window
8. Communal room
9. Bathroom (C)
10. Bedroom (C)
11. Studio
12. Swimming pools
13. Toilet (B)
14. Kitchen/dining room (B)
15. Bedroom (B)

The glass entrance hall in the center of the building is spacious and has 180-degree views. The large French doors slide open automatically to allow the sea breeze to enter the house.

La Isla Beach House

Architect: Juan Carlos Doblado
Location: Playa La Isla, Asia, Cañete, Perú
Photos: © Alex Kornhuber

Despite the house's location in a desert area south of Lima, the weather conditions are not that extreme. The house establishes a relationship between architecture and its surroundings, the desert and the sea.

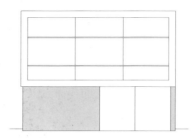

Front elevation

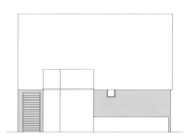

Rear elevation

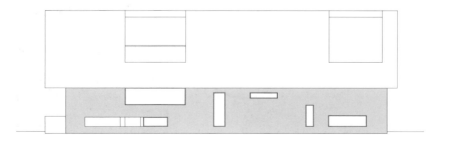

Side elevation

From the outside, the house looks like a juxtaposition of two volumes. The lower level contains the private rooms, and the upper floor—built like a suspended box—houses the public areas and a terrace.

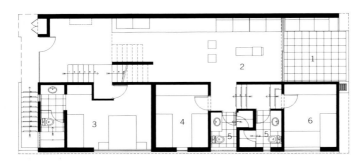

First floor

Second floor

1. Porch
2. Small room
3. Suite
4. Bedroom
5. Bathroom
6. Bedroom
7. Terrace
8. Kitchen
9. Bedroom suite
10. Living room
11. Dining room
12. Swimming pool

White was predominantly used in the building exterior because it reflects the sun in the hot summer months. The terrazzo used in the façade of the first floor adds to the feeling of weightlessness of the upper floor.

Ocean Beach Residence

Architect: Aidlin Darling Design
Location: San Francisco, California, USA
Photos: © Sharon Risendorph

The main objective of this project was to design an extension in keeping with the original building, which was constructed by the architect Ernest Born in the mid-20th century.

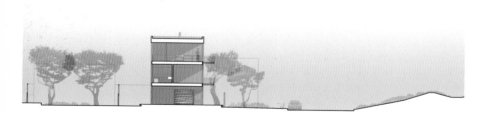

Section

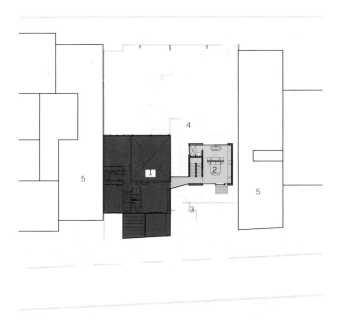

Location map

1. Original building
2. New extension
3. Entrance to the garden
4. Garden
5. Adjacent residence

Separate from the main building, the new extension has three stories and is located in the middle of a small cypress-tree wood. The two buildings are only connected by a glass corridor.

The bathrooms and vertical transit area are in the
north block. The south block has a room for storing
surfboards on the first floor, locker rooms on the
second floor and a fireplace on the rooftop.

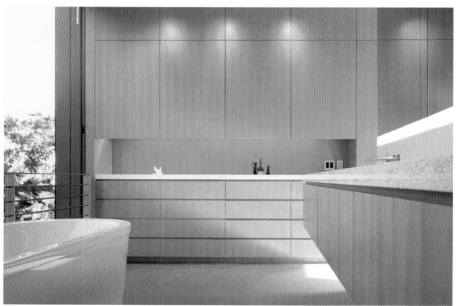

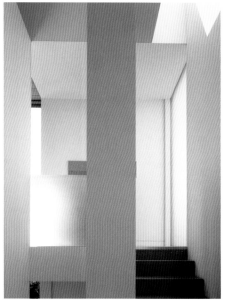

The façade is of Corten steel, a material that is resistant to the harsh coastal climate. Both the original building and extension have managed to maintain their independence while complementing one another.

Ocean Drive Residence

Architect: Stelle Architects
Location: Bridgehampton, New York, USA
Photos: © Jeff Heatley

This project involved building an extension to capitalize on the house's privileged location and spectacular views.

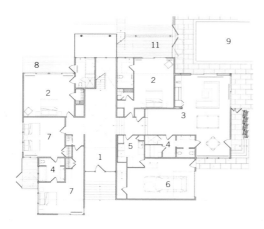

First floor

Second floor

1. Entrance
2. Suite
3. Leisure room
4. Bathroom
5. Laundry room
6. Garage
7. Guest bedroom
8. Covered terrace
9. Swimming pool
10. Living room
11. Dining room
12. Kitchen
13. Larder
14. Guest suite
15. Walk-in closet
16. Bedroom

The house was redesigned to increase the views in all directions. The kitchen, which is part of the new extension, has views of the sea, and the living room and dining room open onto a terrace.

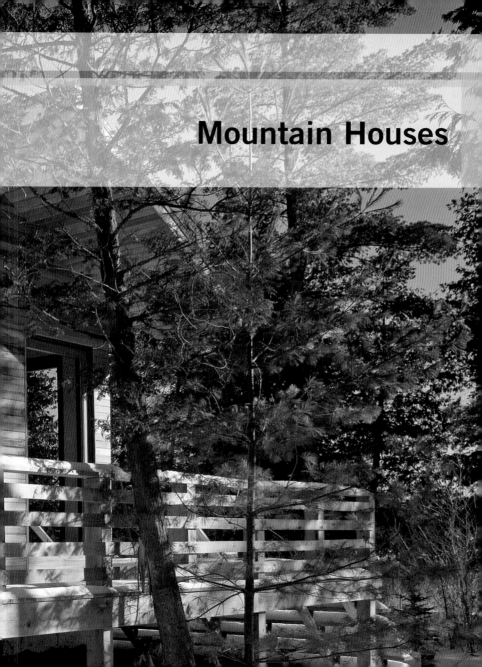

Mountain Houses

Casa Guthrie

Architect: Felipe Assadi & Francisca Pulido
Location: Santiago, Chile
Photos: © Guy Wenborne

This house was commissioned by an estate agent who was looking for a house on a hillside with an average slope of 25 percent. It also had to be within a reasonable budget and not exceed 1,507 sq. ft.

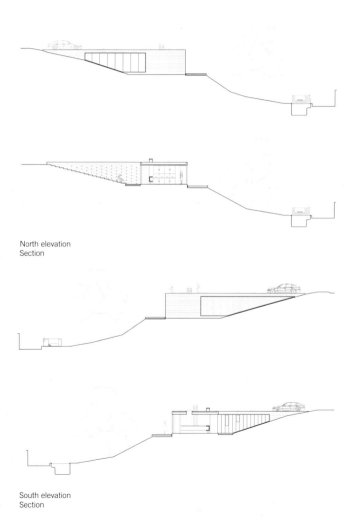

North elevation
Section

South elevation
Section

In an attempt to break away from the massive buildings that abound outside Santiago, the architects designed a house with no façade which looks like a vantage point over Chicureo Valley.

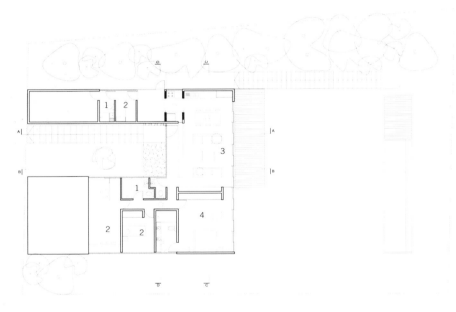

First floor

1. Bathroom
2. Bedroom
3. Living/dining room and kitchen
4. Main suite

The project is a variation on the original assignment and proposes an alternative design that is attractive yet affordable. The problem of the slope was resolved by integrating it into the design.

Lake Seymour Getaway

Architect: UCArchitect
Location: Marmora, Ontario, Canada
Photos: © UCArchitect

Achieving a balance between a feeling of shelter and the need for open space was the challenge posed by this project. The interior is divided into two parts through the use of a central partition.

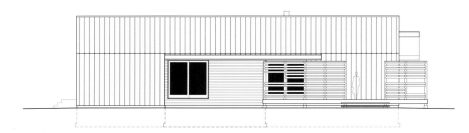

Northwest elevation

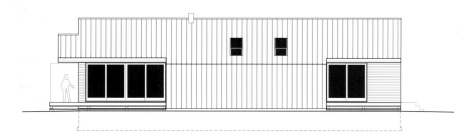

Southeast elevation

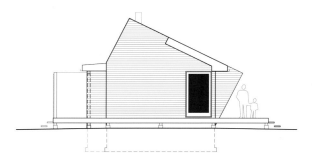

Southwest elevation

The interior spaces are laid out around a nucleus
or box-like structure containing the bathroom and
kitchen. On one side, there is the bedroom and
studio and on the other, the public areas, i.e., the
kitchen, dining room and living room.

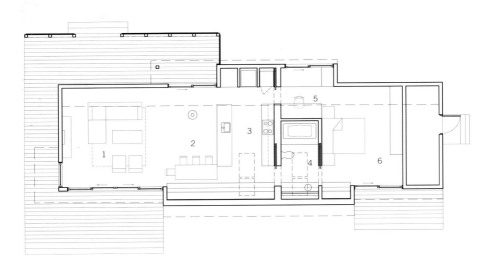

Floor plan

1. Living room
2. Dining room
3. Kitchen
4. Bathroom
5. Studio/bedroom
6. Main bedroom

There are only three doors in the entire building; these are sliding doors and can therefore be opened to create an open space. They are situated in the two corridors on either side of the kitchen and provide access to the bedroom, bathroom and studio.

In addition to the large windows in the communal area, skylights were installed in the roof to ensure that all of the rooms in the house get plenty of natural light.

Spur Lane House

Architect: SPG Architects
Location: Ketchum, Idaho, USA
Photos: © Tim Brown

This house has a concrete and steel structure clad in fir. Thanks to its wooden "skin", the house blends in perfectly with the surrounding landscape.

Basement

First floor

Second floor

1. Garage
2. Toilet
3. Gym
4. Wine cellar
5. Closet
6. Laundry room
7. Lounge
8. Main bedroom
9. Bedroom
10. Bathroom
11. Loft
12. Terrace
13. Living room
14. Dining room
15. Kitchen
16. Terrace dining room
17. Study

The architects placed the garage, gym, engine room and wine cellar in a concrete basement. A staircase leads to the first floor, where the entrance hall and private areas are located.

The bedrooms and bathrooms are located on the first floor, which is quite unusual. The second floor was reserved for the public areas, i.e., the kitchen, living room and dining room, because it has better views.

House Hofmann

Architect: Acn+Architektur
Location: Vienna, Austria
Photos: © Miran Kambič

Overlooking the Wien River Valley and the woods of Vienna, this house has a simple and functional structure: a wooden box inserted into a concrete body.

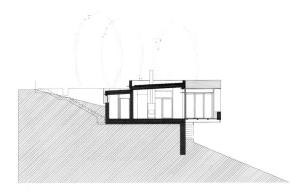

Longitudinal section

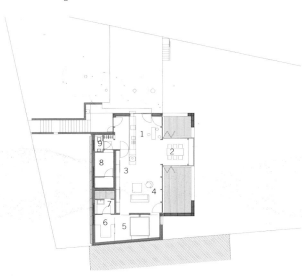

1. Kitchen
2. Dining room
3. Library
4. Living room
5. Bedroom
6. Walk-in closet
7. Bathroom
8. Room
9. Guest bathroom

Floor plan

The prefabricated wooden structure was built on-site. The base is of reinforced concrete and was built on the foundations of the house that was previously on the site.

The concrete body, which is partially sunk in the slope, contains the private areas like the bedroom and bathroom, and supports the wooden structure with steel beams.

Inside the wooden building, the public areas of the house, i.e., the dining room, kitchen and living room, are open-plan and have French doors opening onto two large outdoor patios.

The central part of the house, the block that
contains the kitchen and which ends in a
cylindrical open stove, acts as a passageway
between the hall and private areas of the house.

Residence in Abantos

Architect: Jeff Brock and Belén Moneo/Moneo Brock Studio
Location: San Lorenzo de El Escorial, Madrid, Spain
Photos: © Luis Asín, Jeff Brock

The architects designed a compact structure that is in perfect harmony with the surrounding trees. With views of El Escorial Monastery, the house is laid out around a central glass patio.

Northeast elevation

Northwest elevation

Southeast elevation

Southwest elevation

The first floor follows the shape of the terrain, ensuring that each area has direct access to the exterior, and the terraces become an extension of the house in the garden.

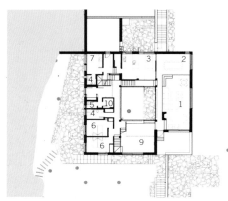

First floor

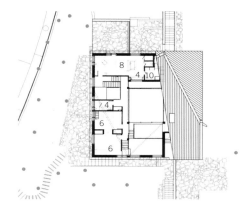

Second floor

1. Living room
2. Dining room
3. Kitchen
4. Bathroom
5. Guest toilet
6. Bedroom
7. Service bedroom
8. Main suite
9. Play room
10. Closet

From the inside and outside, the roof looks like a continuous surface that follows the unevenness of the terrain. The house exterior is compact, while the interior is spacious and open-plan.

On the east, the house is suspended over the foundation, forming a large porch beside the pine trees. As a result, it appears to merge with the landscape and has better views of the monastery.

Humlegård House

Architect: Kimmo Friman/friman.laaksonen
arkkitehdit Oy
Location: Jänvikintie, Fiskars, Finland
Photos: © Rauno Träskelin

This residence is built on a small hill. The north façade faces the cold north winds, while the south façade opens onto the countryside, where white-tailed deers and foxes can often be spotted.

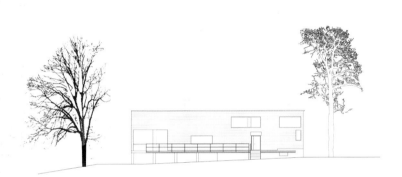

East elevation

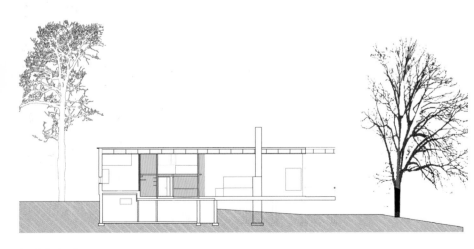

Longitudinal section

The house was built to serve as a home, an area
for entertaining friends and a separate studio. The
interior is comprised of two large rooms connected
by a small loft with a bathroom and a closet on the
first floor.

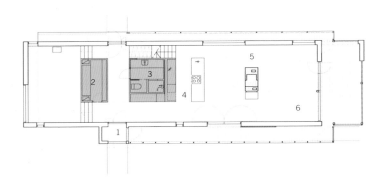

First floor

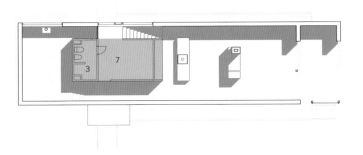

1. Entrance
2. Closet
3. Bathroom
4. Kitchen
5. Dining room
6. Living room
7. Bedroom

Second floor

One of the two areas on the first floor can be used as a bedroom, studio or an extra room; the other contains the kitchen, dining room and living room, which is beside a fireplace and has spectacular views, thanks to the large windows.

A small traditional sauna was built close to the main building and is sheltered by the trees. The warmth of the wood covering the sauna is a sharp contrast to the cold exterior.

Under the Moonlight House

Architect: Studio Giovanni D'Ambrosio
Location: Mount Hotham, Victoria, Australia
Photos: © Peter Mylonas

Typical local materials were used that are part of
the district's historical heritage to make the house
blend in with the rest of the surroundings.

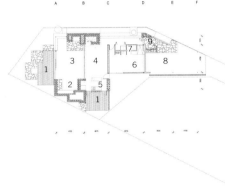

First floor

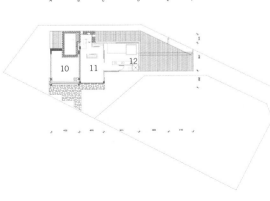

Second floor

1. Terrace
2. Bar
3. Living room
4. Dining room
5. Kitchen
6. Bedroom
7. Bathroom
8. Garage
9. Entrance
10. Hollow
11. Main bedroom
12. Bathroom and spa

The house was designed to ensure the comfort of
the occupants year round and to provide views
of the natural surroundings. This was achieved
thought the use of French doors with generous
views of the exterior.

The house is comprised of two floors. On the first floor are the public areas, which open onto an outdoor terrace, and a bedroom. The main bedroom, with an adjoining bathroom and spa, is located on the second floor.

Ridge House

Architect: Cary Bernstein
Location: Sonoma County, California, USA
Photos: © Sharon Risendorph

This large house is located on a hilltop and was designed to accommodate a family and their guests.

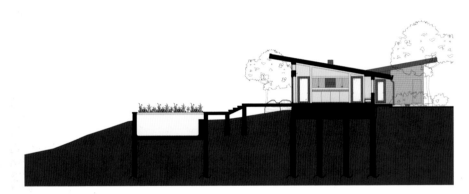

East section

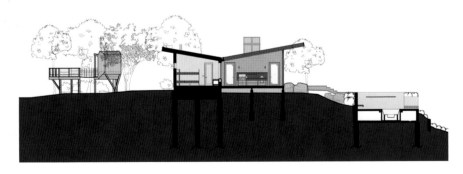

West elevation

All of the rooms open to the exterior to reinforce
the connection with the landscape. Large terraces
and paths provide more space in which to enjoy
time at home.

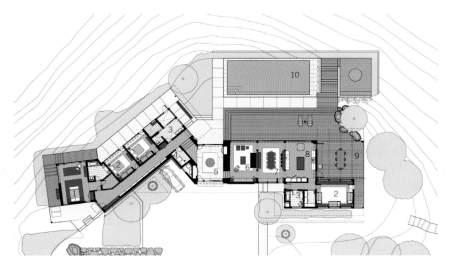

Floor plan

1. Main suite
2. Bedroom
3. Bathroom
4. Laundry room
5. Hall
6. Living room
7. Dining room
8. Kitchen
9. Outdoor dining room
10. Swimming pool

The house is comprised of two wings that start
at the entrance in the center. The public areas
are located in the east wing and have views of the
valley and vineyards; in the west wing are
the bedrooms with views of the woods.

This project considered several ecological aspects, such as the use of recyclable and durable materials like cedar wood, concrete (in the corridors) and porcelain tiles.

Small Houses

Sandou House

Architect: Takaharu & Yui Tezuka/Tezuka
Architects, Masahiro Ikeda/Masahiro Ikeda Co.
Location: Hiroshima, Japan
Photos: © Katsuhisa Kida

This little house is located just 5m from the Seto
Inland Sea in the south of Japan. It has views of
the floating gate or Torii that marks the entrance to
Itsukushima Shrine.

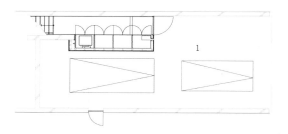

First floor

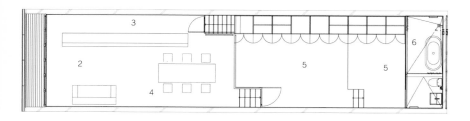

Second floor

1. Garage
2. Living room
3. Kitchen
4. Dining room
5. Bedroom
6. Bathroom

A large front gate protects the house from typhoons and, when open, establishes a link between the interior and exterior. The terraced floor ensures that most of the rooms have views.

Home Front to an Island

Architect: Juan Carlos Doblado
Location: Playa La Isla, Cañete, Perú
Photos: © Elsa Ramírez

This house overlooks the Pacific Ocean and occupies all of the permitted building area. It is comprised of just two floors: a basement and a spacious first floor.

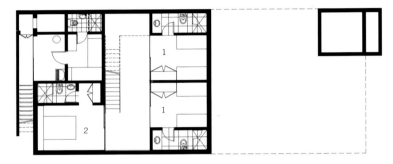

Basement

1. Bedroom with bathroom
2. Double bedroom with bathroom
3. Main bedroom
4. Guest bathroom
5. Kitchen
6. Living/dining room
7. Small room

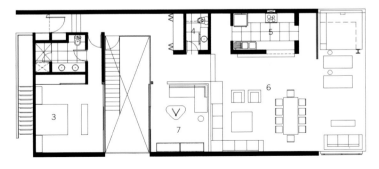

First floor

From the outside, the house has a sleek form, with a patio at the basement level. The roof protrudes beyond the main façade, forming a porch of the same size as the overhang.

Sea Ranch Residence

Architect: Eric Haesloop, Mary Griffin/Turnbull
Griffin Haesloop
Location: The Sea Ranch, California, USA
Photos: © David Wakely, Jim Alinder

The Pacific Ocean bathes the coastline where this residence is located (about 6.2 miles north of San Francisco, in a perfect spot for holiday breaks).

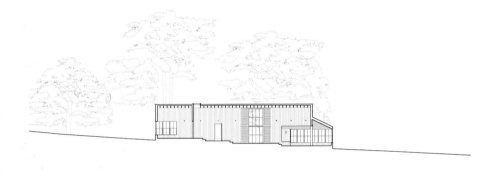

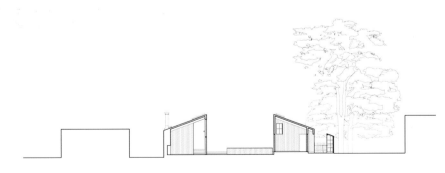

Elevations

The main bedroom and bathroom are separate from the rest of the house. It therefore has two separate structures that frame the views and make the landscape the center of attention.

The main building contains the public areas, such as the kitchen, dining room and living room, as well as a bathroom and bedroom. An outdoor dining room was built on a wooden platform between the two buildings.

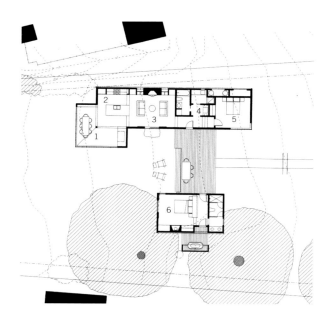

Floor plan

1. Dining room
2. Kitchen
3. Living room
4. Bathroom
5. Bedroom
6. Main suite

GP House

Architect: exe.arquitectura
Location: Riudarenes, Girona, Spain
Photos: © Lluís Sans

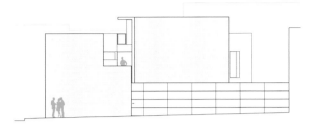

Southeast elevation

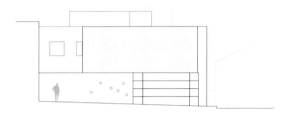

Northeast elevation

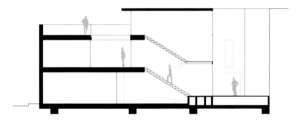

Longitudinal section

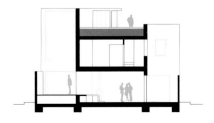

Transverse section

From the outset, this project was subject to strict planning rules regarding height, materials, and the layout of windows and doors to ensure that it would fit in with the other houses in the village.

The solid and simple façade contrasts sharply
with the interior, which has large windows onto
the interior courtyards to ensure that the house
receives plenty of natural light.

First floor

Second floor

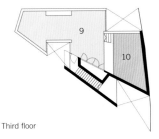

Third floor

1. Garage
2. Guest bathroom
3. Kitchen
4. Living/dining room
5. Bedroom
6. Bathroom
7. Studio
8. Main bedroom
9. Solarium
10. Swimming pool

The garage, kitchen, living room, dining room and a bathroom are located on the first floor. The second floor contains two bedrooms with walk-in closets and bathrooms, and a studio. A small swimming pool and solarium were built on the rooftop.

Green Houses

Ehrlich Residence

Architect: John Friedman and Alice Kimm
Architects
Location: Santa Monica, California, USA
Photos: © Luc Roymans

The main objectives of this project were to design a sustainable home with continuous space, to make the most of the natural light and to establish a close link between the interior and exterior.

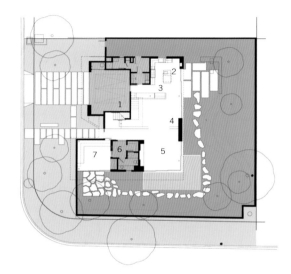

1. Service areas
2. Kitchen
3. Larder
4. Dining room
5. Living room
6. Bathroom
7. Study and guest bedroom
8. Bedroom
9. Main bedroom
10. Main bathroom

First floor

Second floor

Rooftops

The occupants were determined to make the most of the south façade so as to take advantage of the sunlight in winter and to enable cross ventilation in the hot summer months.

The house is lined with plaster and cement panels
in natural tones. The wood used in the door,
staircases and third floor is from sustainable forests.

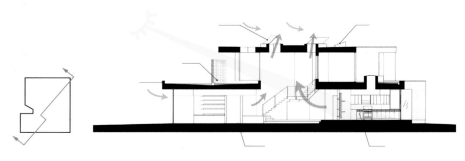

Bioclimatic section

The central atrium acts as a "solar" chimney in summer. Hot air is expelled through the automatic gates which also suck in fresh air. The photovoltaic system on the roof meets 85 percent of the house's energy requirements.

Annie Residence

Architect: Bercy Chen Studio
Location: Austin, Texas, USA
Photos: © Mike Osborne, Joseph Pettyjohn

This project is a good example of sustainable and ecological architecture in terms of the materials used and the construction process. The house is comprised of two wings connected by a glass corridor.

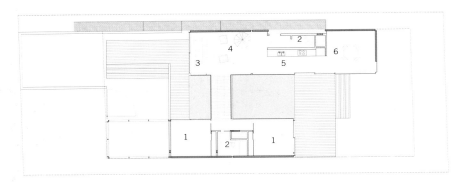

First floor

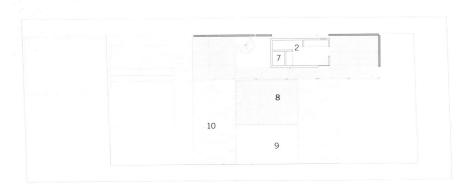

Second floor

1. Bedroom
2. Bathroom
3. Living room
4. Spiral staircase
5. Kitchen
6. Dining room
7. Closet
8. Reflecting pool
9. Roof
10. Deck

Each wing has a central nucleus comprised of a steel structure that contains the public areas. The swimming pool is the focal point of the project and all of the rooms in the house are laid out around it.

The frame of the building is comprised of a single steel shell clad in precast panels, which reduced the time required to complete the project. This shell is exposed and joins the façades of the house.

The rooftops were converted into large terraces where the occupants can enjoy the fresh air. The folding canvas awning provides shade so that the area can also be used as an outdoor dining room.

Heathdale House

Architect: Teeple Architects
Location: Toronto, Ontario
Photos: © Tom Arban

Given the location of this house—on a long lot closely flanked by other houses—the architects were charged with finding ways of capitalizing on the available space.

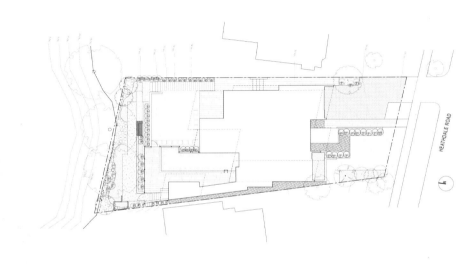

Location map

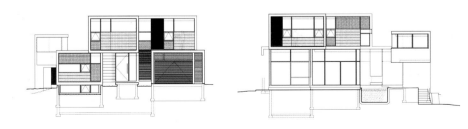

South elevation

North elevation

The house consists of a number of boxes piled into two stories. The disorderly layout of the boxes enabled the installation of several windows and glass panels in place of exterior walls.

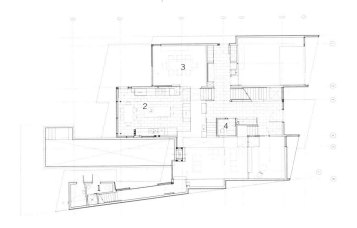

First floor

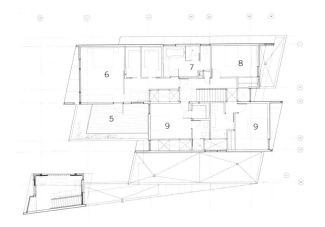

1. Guest bathroom
2. Kitchen/dining room
3. Covered outdoor dining room
4. Bathroom
5. Terrace
6. Bedroom
7. Bathroom
8. Bedroom
9. Suite

Second floor

The exterior is clad in materials like sealed wood, dyed cedar and zinc panels. The boxes are of wood, which is also used in the interior to reinforce the idea of a work of sculpture.

TDA House

Architect: Eduardo Cadaval & Clara
Solà-Morales
Location: Puerto Escondido, Oaxaca, México
Photos: © Santiago Garcés, Cadaval
Solà-Morales

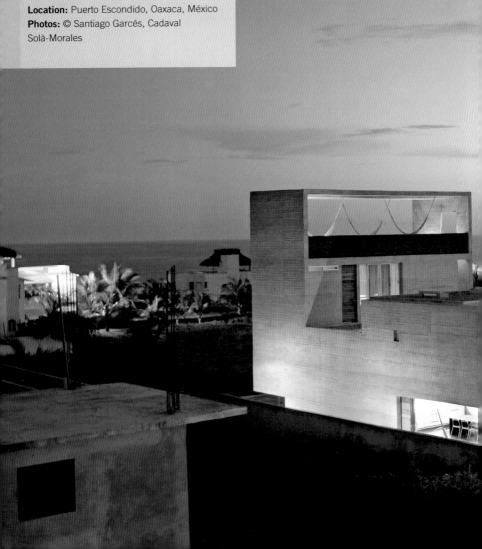

This house could be described as a concrete box comprised of three structures. The objective was to avoid the high temperatures of the Mexican coast and to keep the interior cool by opening the building to the exterior.

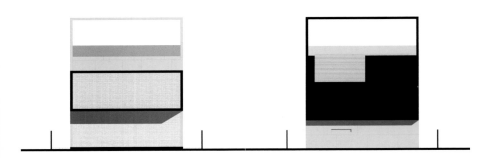

North elevation

South elevation

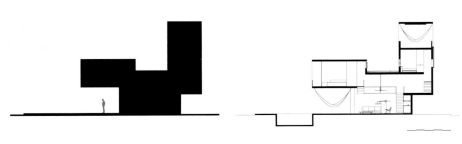

East elevation

Longitudinal section

Beside the swimming pool and under a suspended structure, is one of the most interesting rooms in the house. Despite its exterior location, it is close to the public areas and sheltered.

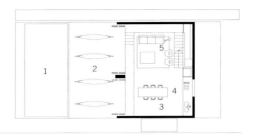

First floor

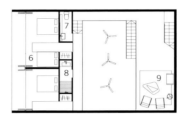

Second floor

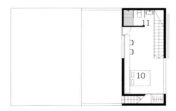

Third floor

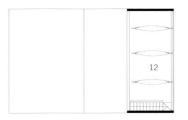

Roof terrace

1. Swimming pool
2. Porch
3. Dining room
4. Kitchen
5. Living room
6. Bedroom
7. Toilet
8. Bathroom
9. Lounge
10. Main bedroom
11. Bathroom
12. Terrace

The house is comprised of three bodies. The first is a tower that rises into the sky in search of sea views; the second consists of several rooms that are suspended over the garden and swimming pool; and the third is a central area and hallway.

A vantage point with panoramic views of the Pacific Ocean was built on the highest point of the house. Red hammocks were hung there so that the occupants could enjoy the views in greater comfort and to give the house personality.

Villa Lena

Architect: Olavi Koponen
Location: Nesodden, Espoo, Finland
Photos: © Jussi Tiainen

This house was laid out in a single open space. The gardens act as a mediator between nature and the building, which is protected from prying eyes on the street.

North elevation

South elevation

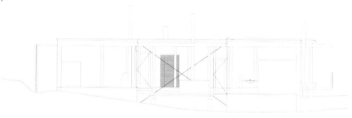

West elevation

East elevation

In the interior, the different rooms are not clearly defined or separated. Thin curtains and the occasional object indicate the separations between the different rooms.

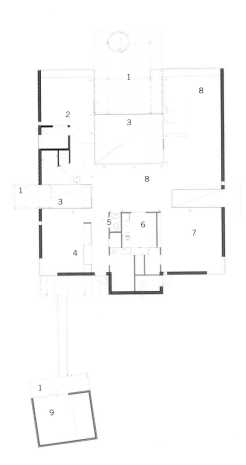

Floor plan

1. Patio
2. Suite
3. Garden
4. Bedroom
5. Bathroom
6. Kitchen
7. Bedroom
8. Living/dining room
9. Studio

The interior walls and ceilings are of tongued and grooved timber. The floors are of polished concrete mixed with broken glass.

The façade is clad in weather-resistant Siberian larch. Rockwool was used for insulation and the windows are equipped with energy-saving devices.

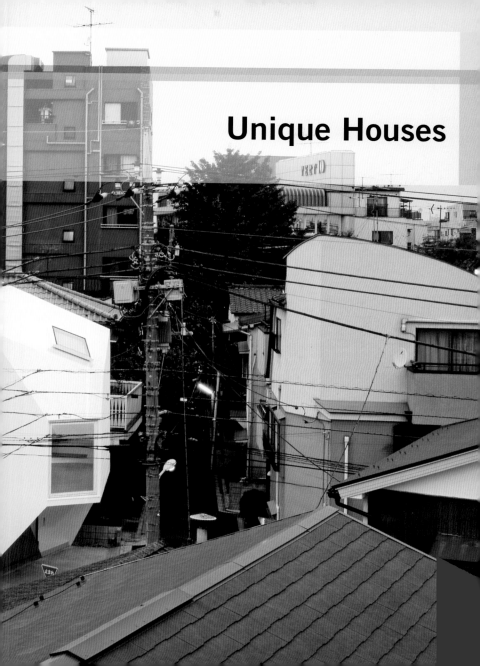

Unique Houses

Xeros Residence

Architect: Blank Studio
Location: Phoenix, Arizona, USA
Photos: © Bill Timmerman

The house has views of the natural reserve on the north and the city of Phoenix on the south. It consists of a duplex with a study on the ground level and the living quarters on the second floor.

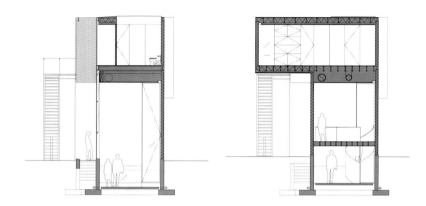

Transverse sections

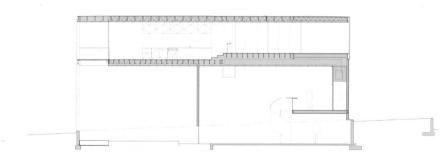

Longitudinal section

The house is accessed by an exterior steel staircase that leads to a small balcony which in turn leads to the public areas. After crossing a gallery, you arrive at the main bedroom and a game room.

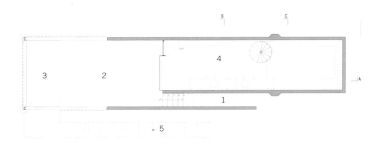

First floor

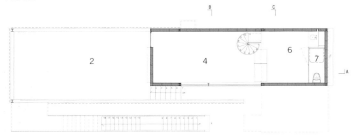

Second floor

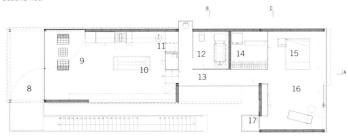

Third floor

1. Studio entrance
2. Outdoor patio
3. Swimming pool
4. Studio
5. House entrance
6. Library
7. Guest bathroom
8. Terrace
9. Living room
10. Dining room
11. Kitchen
12. Bathroom
13. Gallery
14. Walk-in closet
15. Bedroom
16. Game room
17. Romeo and Juliet balcony

The private area of the house has a large glass window on the north with views of the mountains. In addition, the Romeo and Juliet balcony—in yellow glass—offers a panoramic view of the city.

The main material is exposed steel, which was used both in the structure and façade. Transparent glass was used in the windows and French doors and yellow tinted glass in the balcony. Fair-faced concrete was also used in the interior of the studio.

Reflection of Mineral

Architect: Yasuhiro Yamashita and Yoichi Tanaka/Atelier Tekuto
Location: Nakano, Tokyo, Japan
Photos: © Makoto Yoshida

This small area of just 474 sq. ft. occupies the corner of a lot on which the architects decided to build a polygonal single-family house. The house is comprised of four floors with a total area of 925 sq. ft.

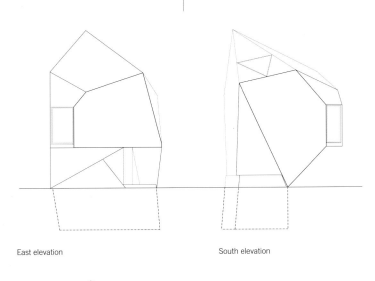

East elevation

South elevation

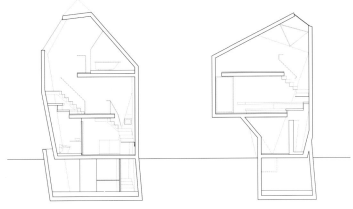

West section

North section

The name of the project was inspired by its angular shape, which is reminiscent of a partially buried mineral. Because of the irregular design, the light penetrates into the house in different ways depending on the time of day, thus creating different effects.

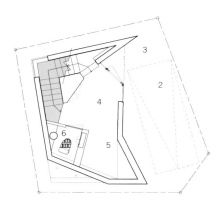

First floor

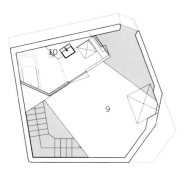

Third floor

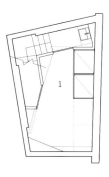

Basement

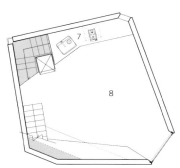

Second floor

1. Bedroom
2. Garage
3. Porch
4. Hall
5. Closet
6. Guest bathroom
7. Kitchen
8. Living/dining room
9. Laundry room
10. Bathroom

A rigid, reinforced concrete frame was built to create the polygonal shape and to gain living space. There was also sufficient space to build an indoor garage.

In the basement of the house is the bedroom; the bathroom and entrance hall are on the first floor; the kitchen, dining room and bathroom are on the second floor; and on the third floor there is an open space with a bathtub.

Deck House

Architect: Felipe Assadi & Francisca Pulido
Location: Alto Runge, Chile
Photos: © Guy Wenborne

The focal point of this project is the wooden panel comprising the spacious terrace (complete with swimming pool) which ascends until completely surrounding the house.

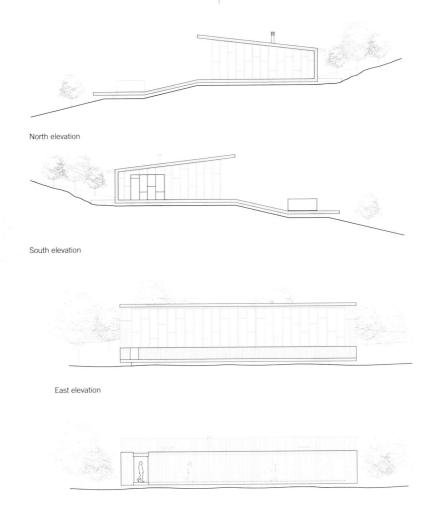

North elevation

South elevation

East elevation

West elevation

It was decided to turn this terrace into a "stage"
from which to enjoy the magnificent views. Large
glass windows were installed in most of the
enclosed structure.

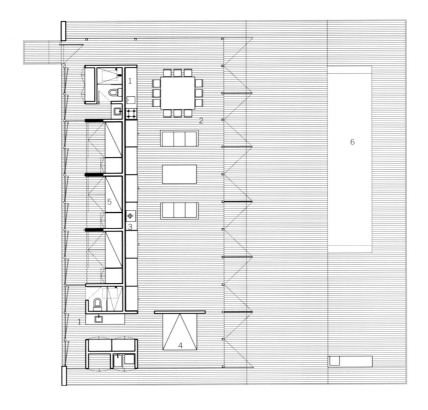

Floor plan

1. Bathroom
2. Living/dining room
3. Kitchen
4. Main bedroom
5. Small bedrooms
6. Swimming pool

The public areas in the interior are arranged in an open-plan style. The floor was divided lengthways through the use of a wall with a built-in kitchen, bathrooms and several small bedrooms. At one end of the house, is the main bedroom.

On the other side of the kitchen, and built into the partition wall, there are several very small single bedrooms that are just large enough to sleep in. The idea was to save space for the public areas.

Triangle House

Architect: Jarmund/ Vigsnæs AS Architects MNAL
Location: Nesodden, Norway
Photos: © Ivan Brodey

The architects had to design a triangular building because of the shape of the lot. The house has magnificent views of the Oslo fjord through the tree branches.

Northwest elevation

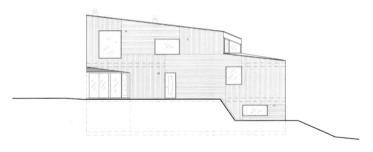

South elevation

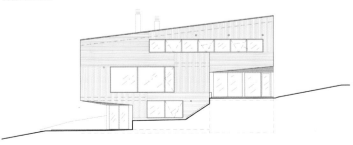

East elevation

The unusual layout of the windows—in different shapes and sizes—catches the attention of the viewer from the outside. In the interior, the public areas are laid out in an open-plan style.

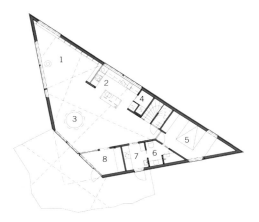

First floor

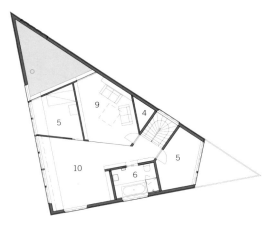

Second floor

1. Library lounge with a double-height ceiling
2. Kitchen
3. Dining room
4. Storage space
5. Bedroom
6. Bathroom
7. Laundry room
8. Hall
9. Living room/Guests
10. Study

The exterior wall is clad in wooden panels positioned the same as the windows. Inside, the floors are of concrete and partially covered with sisal mats.

House Kotilo

Architect: Olavi Koponen
Location: Espoo, Finland
Photos: © Jussi Tiainen

Inspired by an interview with the Finnish film
director Aki Kaurismäki, Olavi Koponen designed
this house in the shape of a spiral built around
a fireplace.

Second floor

First floor

1. Bedroom
2. Bathroom
3. Living room
4. Kitchen
5. Loft suite

The shape of the house enabled the architect to experiment with space and play with the light as it changes throughout the day and year. The objective was to achieve privacy, naturalness and simplicity.

The basic structure—with prefabricated wooden floors, walls and ceilings—revolves around a central concrete fireplace, partially supported by steel pillars.

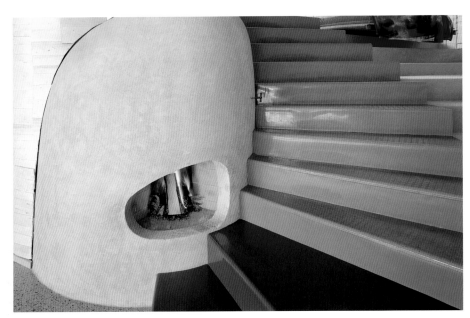

Amalia House

Architect: GRID Architekten
Location: Sytria, Austria
Photos: © Lukas Schaller

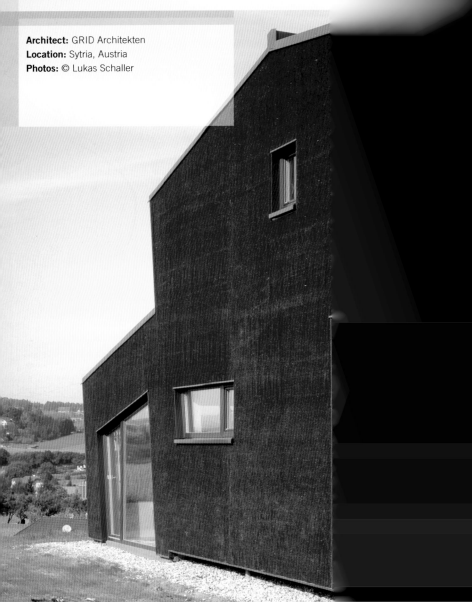

This project was commissioned by three siblings who wanted to have a second home close to their parents. The only requirements were low cost and enough space for six people.

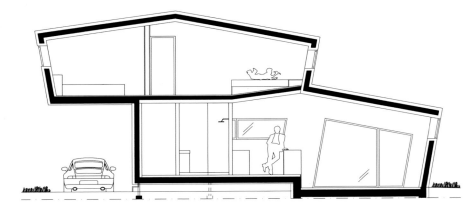

Longitudinal section

The two-story building is located on a hilltop. It has a peculiar angular and irregular shape and includes an overhang structure on the second floor.

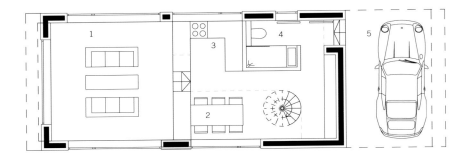

First floor

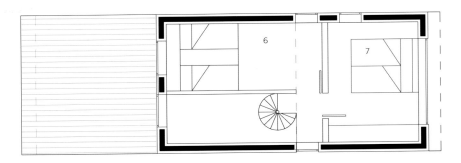

Second floor

1. Living room
2. Dining room
3. Kitchen
4. Bathroom
5. Garage
6. Bedroom
7. Main bedroom

As a tribute to the natural surrounding and to establish a dialogue between the interior and exterior, all of the façade, except for the windows, was covered in artificial grass.

Two French doors on the first floor constitute the main entrance, ensuring that the interior gets plenty of natural light and that the landscape forms part of the house and vice versa.

On the lower floor, where the public areas and bathroom are located, the living room is separated from the kitchen and dining room by a step. This divides the different areas without the need for partitions.

Kuro House

Architect: Hiromasa Mori & Takuya
Hosokai/1980
Location: Fukui, Japan
Photos: © 1980

The structure of this house is of wood and the
exterior walls are also of dark wood, which is where
it gets its name *Kuro*, meaning black in Japanese.

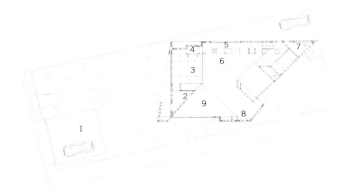

First floor

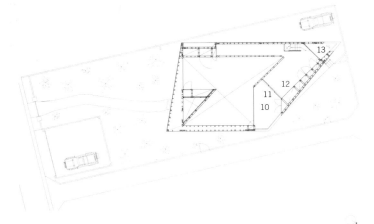

Second floor

1. Garage
2. Entrance
3. Japanese room
4. Buddhist altar
5. Kitchen
6. Dining room
7. Patio
8. Desks
9. Living room
10. Terrace
11. Utility room
12. Study
13. Court yard

One of the vertexes of the building extends to the front of the lot forming a sharp angle. The house has an area of 1,744 sq. ft. and was built in a traditional Japanese garden.

This experimental residence was built for a couple.
Because the different rooms did not need to be
separated, only discreet partitions were used.

Prefab Houses

Sunset Cabin

Architect: Taylor Smyth Architects
Location: Lake Simcoe, Ontario, Canada
Photos: © Ben Rahn/A-Frame, Taylor Smyth
Architects

This small cabin is the perfect place to escape from it all, even from the nearby holiday home. It has an area of 323 sq. ft. and includes just a bedroom, bathroom and fireplace.

Location map

This glass box was covered with horizontal cedar panels. These are cut at the east side and disappear towards the north, which is the best side from which to watch the sun set over the lake.

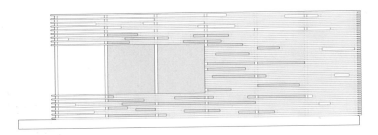

East elevation

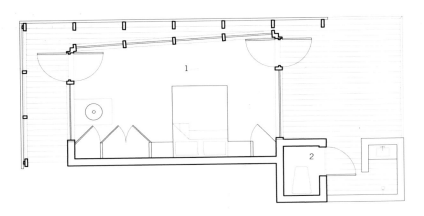

Floor plan

1. Bedroom
2. Bathroom

The difficulty of working in a remote area with a slope was resolved by purchasing a pre-fabricated house in Toronto. The house was dismantled piece by piece and reassembled on the desired site in just ten days.

Modular 4

Architect: Studio 804
Location: Kansas City, Kansas, USA
Photos: © Studio 804

Speed, quality construction and affordable prices characterize these prefabricated houses. One, two or three bedrooms can be formed simply by moving the closets that serve as partition walls.

Floor with three bedrooms

1. Kitchen/dining room
2. Bathroom
3. Bedroom

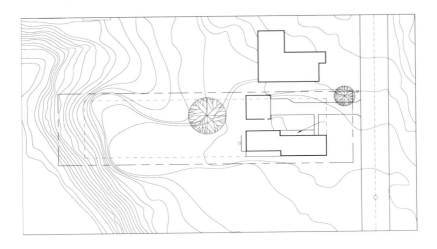

Open floor plan

The only fixed walls in the interior were laid out in parallel lines. These include the main and guest bathroom walls and the walls of the kitchen and laundry room.

Most of the house was built in a warehouse and then transported to its final destination. Recycled materials were used in the foundations and other elements of the home.

X House

Architect: Adrián Moreno, María Samaniego/
Arquitectura X
Location: La Tola, Quito, Ecuador
Photos: © Sebastián Crespo

This home was designed before a site had been chosen for its location. After much consideration, an open box-like structure made of glass was created to provide the feeling of unlimited space.

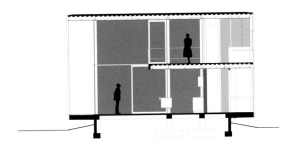

Transverse section

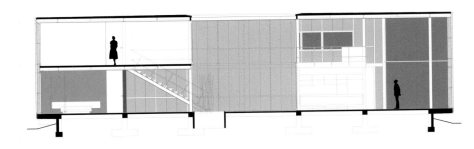

Longitudinal section

The public and private areas are separated
by a patio—one of the focal points of the
project—behind which there is a corridor.

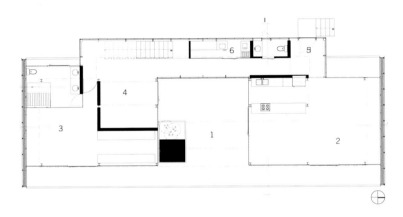

First floor

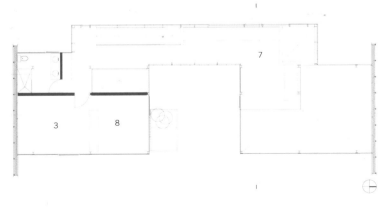

Second floor

1. Patio
2. Living/dining
   room and
   kitchen
3. Bedroom
4. Family room
5. Entrance
6. Guest bathroom
7. Studio/library
8. Playroom

A modular construction system can be adapted to different budgets and locations. A steel structure with a concrete foundation and base supports an open box of lacquered plywood and rusted varnished steel.

House on the Lake

Architect: Michael Meredith, Hilary Sample/MOS
Location: Lake Huron, Ontario, Canada
Photos: © Florian Holzherr

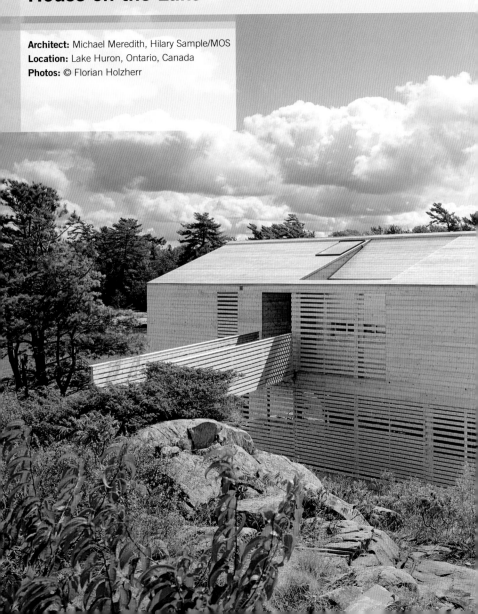

This house is built on Lake Huron. Given the special conditions of the location, the project had to meet very specific needs while preserving the architectural style of a typical local house.

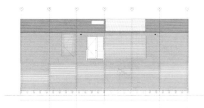

North elevation

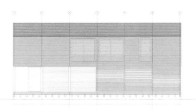

South elevation

East elevation

West elevation

Its unusual location posed many challenges for the manufacture and construction of the house as the whole process could not be carried out on the location itself.

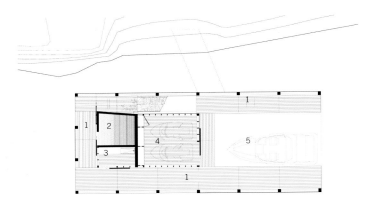

First floor

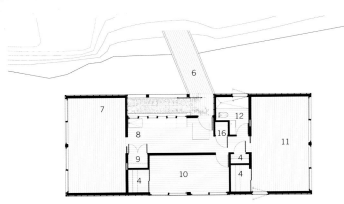

Second floor

1. Wharf
2. Sauna
3. Laundry room
4. Storage space
5. Open space
6. Bridge
7. Living room
8. Kitchen
9. Larder
10. Study
11. Bedroom
12. Bathroom

The water level changes constantly, varying with the seasons. To overcome this problem, the house was placed on a steel platform supported by pontoons, allowing the water level to fluctuate naturally.

Because the cost of transporting the platform
would have been very high, it was assembled by a
local company and then towed to the lakeside
where the house was built and eventually anchored
in the lake.

The façade is clad in cedar boards; small windows were installed to allow the light to penetrate to the interior while protecting it from prying eyes.

Minimalist Houses

House in Cologne

Architect: Martin Schneider
Location: Cologne, Germany
Photos: © Cornelis Gollhardt

This house is comprised of shiny white cubes
that contrast with the lush vegetation and trees
surrounding the lot.

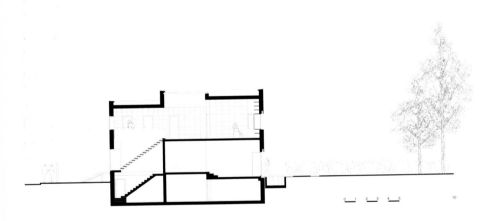

Section

0 1 2 3 4 5   10

The many windows connect the interior with the
exterior. These have no frames on the inside to
create the impression of landscape paintings.

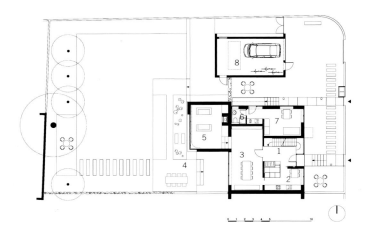

First floor

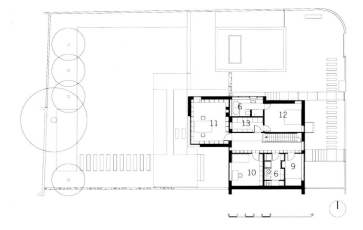

1. Entrance
2. Kitchen
3. Dining room
4. Outdoor dining room
5. Living room
6. Bathroom
7. Small apartment
8. Garage
9. Bedroom
10. Library
11. Studio
12. Main bedroom
13. Walk-in closet

Second floor

The windows do have frames on the outside, however, to create the impression of paintings on white canvas. The large French doors beside the living and dining rooms open onto the patio and garden.

A large green cube was placed between the kitchen, dining room and hall to separate them and to hold a closet, the kitchen cupboards and other storage units.

A large skylight was installed over the stairs leading to the upper floor to provide extra light. Beside the stairs and running the length of the wall are bookshelves lining the way to the library.

Wolf House

Architect: Pezo von Ellrichshausen Architects
Location: Andalue, Chile
Photos: © Cristóbal Palma

Most of the houses in this part of Chile have an attic to make up for the living space restrictions imposed by the Housing Plan.

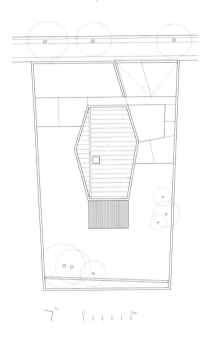

Location map

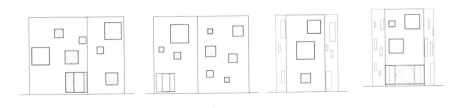

North elevation

South elevation

West elevation

East elevation

The public areas are laid out in an open-plan style on the first or ground floor of the building. The living room is beside a paved terrace and the kitchen is at the opposite wall, with a space in between for the dining room.

First floor

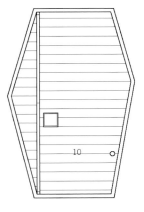

Second floor

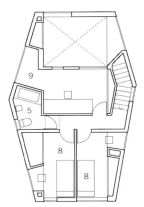

Third floor

Roof

1. Living room
2. Guest bathroom
3. Dining room
4. Kitchen
5. Bathroom
6. Main bedroom
7. Walk-in closet
8. Bedroom
9. Studio
10. Roof

The second floor was devoted exclusively to the main bedroom, a bathroom and a spacious walk-in closet. An empty space looks onto the living room, giving it a double-height ceiling.

The rest of the bedrooms and a studio are located on the third floor. The exterior wall cladding has a uniform texture that flows in the direction of the rain, and has windows of different sizes.

CI House

Architect: Paul Cha
Location: Germantown, New York, USA
Photos: © Dao-Lou Zha

This house consists of a two-story rectangular building. The first floor has a height of 10.8 ft. and the second, where the private rooms are located, 8.9 ft. Concrete foundations support the wooden structure.

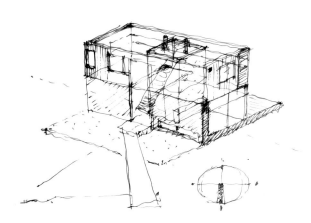

Sketch

North elevation

West elevation

South elevation

East elevation

The façade with the main door is of concrete to the first floor; and the upper part is of wood, with large windows.

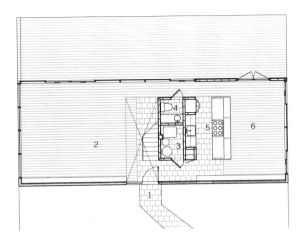

First floor

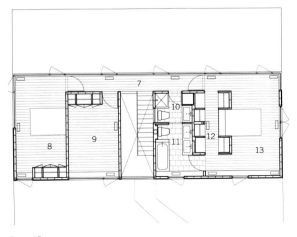

Second floor

1. Entrance
2. Living room
3. Storage room
4. Guest bathroom
5. Kitchen
6. Dining room
7. Hallway
8. Bedroom
9. Studio
10. Guest bathroom
11. Main bathroom
12. Walk-in closet
13. Main bedroom

The first floor is laid out around a central nucleus of a storage room, guest bathroom and kitchen. This nucleus separates the living room and dining room, situated on either end of the building.

The second floor is laid out in the same way, with
the central nucleus of the guest bathroom,
main bedroom and closet; the rest of the space
is devoted to the bedrooms and a study.

VH-R10 gHouse

Architect: Darren Petrucci
Location: Vineyard Haven, Massachusetts, USA
Photos: © Bill Timmerman

Despite its curious name and large dimensions, this project is actually a guest house on the famous island of Martha's Vineyard on the coast of Massachusetts.

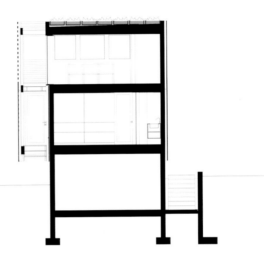

Transverse section

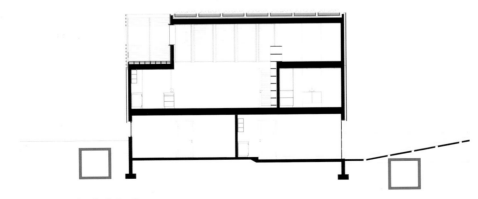

Longitudinal section

The island is famous for its strong winds and strict local planning restrictions, which the architect took into account when designing the project.

The house, custom built for the architect and his wife, is a compact and simple block. It features modern materials and furniture with plenty of personal touches.

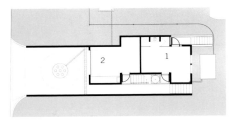

Basement

First floor

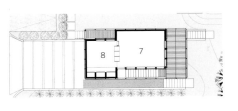

Second floor

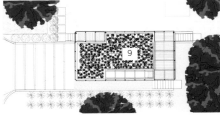

Third floor

1. Guest bedroom
2. Garage
3. Hall
4. Living/dining room
5. Kitchen
6. Suite
7. Open space
8. Studio
9. Roof garden

The kitchen, living room and main bedroom are located on the first floor and have large windows and panels to protect them from the elements. The studio is located on the floor above and looks onto the living room, with a staircase connecting the two levels.

A garden was built on the rooftop to reduce the heat absorbed by the interior and to visually connect the building and its surroundings.

White House

Architect: Jarmund/Vigsnæs AS Architects
MNAL
Location: Strand, Norway
Photos: © Ivan Brodey

This sleek ultra-modern building in white is a sharp contrast to the green landscape of this suburb in Strand and the surrounding rustic buildings.

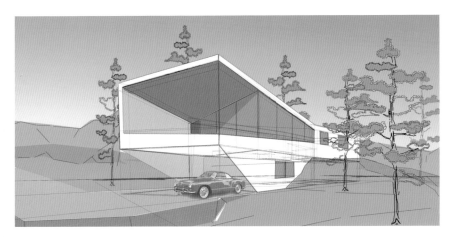

Perspective

Longitudinal section

The interior and exterior are clad in white wooden panels. The walls and ceilings of the second floor have an oak finish, while the floor and walls of the first floor are concrete.

North elevation

South elevation

East elevation

West elevation

The irregular-shaped façade was designed to open the house up to the exterior to visually connect it with the surroundings while preserving the occupants' privacy.

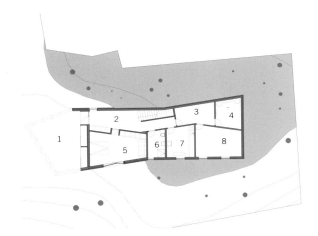

First floor

1. Garage
2. Entrance
3. Storage space
4. Games room
5. Bedroom
6. Bathroom
7. Laundry room
8. Workshop
9. Terrace
10. Dining room
11. Kitchen
12. Living room

Second floor

Oak painted white, pale-colored wood, large windows and simple furniture give this home a minimalist, modern and cozy feel.

The Six

Architect: Ibarra Rosano Design Architects
Location: Tucson, Arizona, USA
Photos: © Bill Timmerman

This project is comprised of five houses with an interior patio. The residential complex is located in a neighborhood in Tucson and is surrounded by trees that provide ample shade.

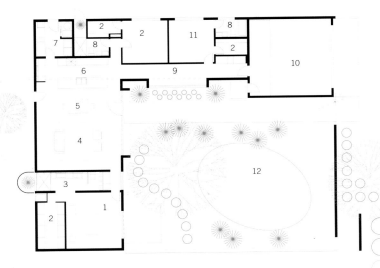

Floor plan

1. Main bedroom
2. Closet
3. Main bathroom
4. Living room
5. Dining room
6. Kitchen
7. Laundry room
8. Bathroom
9. Gallery
10. Garage
11. Bedroom
12. Central patio

The house opens onto a central patio, which connects the interior and exterior, while preserving the privacy of the innermost rooms.

Painted concrete, glass, steel, aluminum and wood were used to create a warm and elegant atmosphere. Several energy-saving systems ensure the comfort of the house's inhabitants.

Because the ceiling of the kitchen is higher than
the rest of the house, skylights were installed to
ensure that natural light reaches the dining room
and living room.

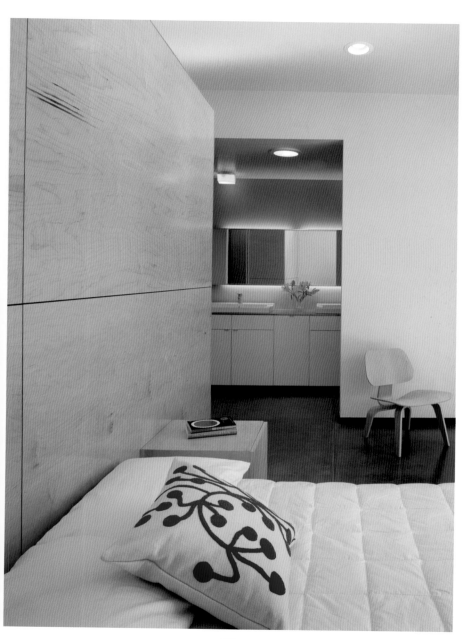

McLaren House

Architect: MacKay-Lyons Sweetapple Architects
Location: St Margaret's Bay, Nova Scotia, Canada
Photos: © James Steeves

This four-story house has a guest bedroom and a
study on the first floor. The bedrooms are located
on the third floor and the public areas on
the fourth.

First floor

Second floor

Third floor

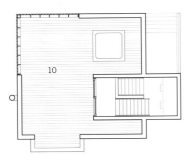

Roof

1. Hall
2. Toilet
3. Study
4. Guest bedroom
5. Main bedroom
6. Children's bedroom
7. Laundry room
8. Bathroom
9. Living/dining room and kitchen
10. Roof

Wood has mainly been used to create a cozy
atmosphere in this house, which peeps out from
among the trees as if searching for the sun.
On the top floor there is a large terrace with
magnificent views.

Renovated Houses

The Barn House

Architect: BURO II/BURO Interior
Location: Central West Flanders, Belgium
Photos: © Danica Ocvirk Kus, Kris Vandamme

Tradition, innovation and respect for the environment are combined in this project, which involved converting an old barn into a home. The topography of the land and the harsh weather conditions in the area were taken into consideration when designing it.

Front elevation

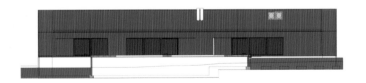

Rear elevation

Side elevations

One of the objectives when designing the house was to maintain a connection and harmony between the landscape and the architecture. There are two large windows at either end of the house to enhance this interaction.

Second floor

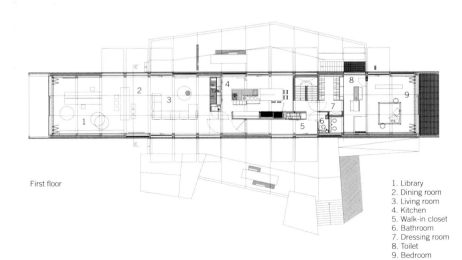

First floor

1. Library
2. Dining room
3. Living room
4. Kitchen
5. Walk-in closet
6. Bathroom
7. Dressing room
8. Toilet
9. Bedroom

Except for the large windows on either end of the house, it is otherwise airtight in order to protect it from adverse weather conditions. Nevertheless, the side walls are mobile and can be opened on sunny days.

Alan-Voo Family House

Architect: Neil M. Denari Architects
Location: Miami Beach, Florida, USA
Photos: © Benny Chan

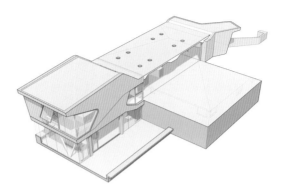

Axonometric plan

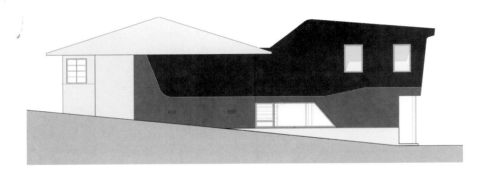

North elevation

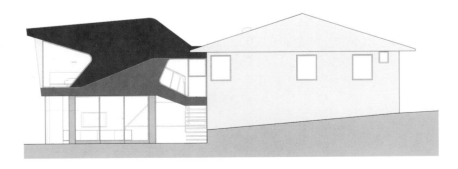

South elevation

A glass box was added to one end of this house in order to enlarge it and to give it a much more original and modern look. The living room was built on the lower floor of the glass structure and the main suite on the upper floor.

After building the extension, the old part of the house was converted into three bedrooms for the owners' daughters and the extension was used for the public areas.

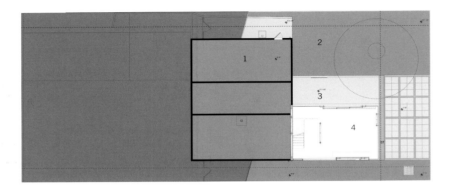

Lower level

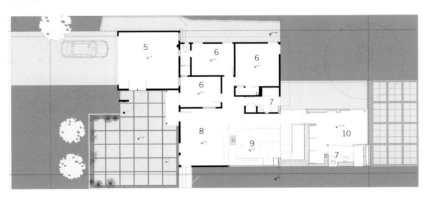

First floor

1. Basement
2. Grass garden
3. Concrete patio
4. Living room
5. Garage
6. Single bedroom
7. Bathroom
8. Dining room
9. Kitchen
10. Main bedroom

The new extension has large glass windows and open-plan spaces in order to make the most of the natural light. Nevertheless, it maintains its privacy because the new rooms look onto a private garden.

Lilyfield House

Architect: Nobbs Radford Architects
Location: Sydney, Australia
Photos: © Murray Frederiks

The appearance of the original building—clad in wood—was maintained and the new extension is a reinterpretation of a two-story cabin.

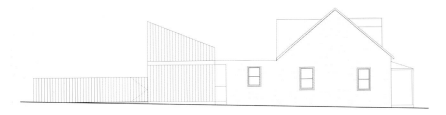

South elevation

East elevation

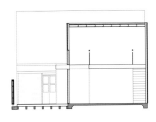

Transverse section

Instead of using horizontal wooden boards, steel
sheets were positioned vertically to adorn the
façade. The green strip is a continuation of
the ceiling of the first floor.

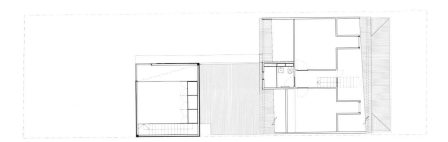

First floor

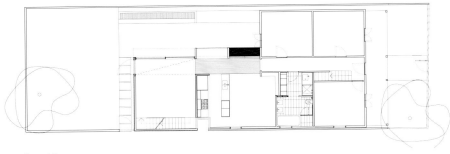

Second floor

The new extension contains the living room with a
children's loft, a study corner, kitchen and
dining room.

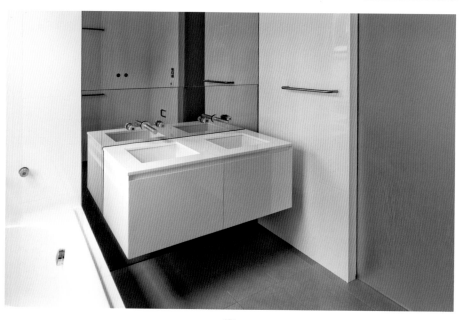

Beverly Skyline Residence

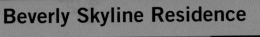

Architect: Bercy Chen Studio
Location: Austin, Texas, USA
Photos: © Ryan Michael, Joseph Pettyjohn

This project involved building an extension to a house that was constructed in the 1970s and renovating the interior. The main objective was to take advantage of the steep terrain to obtain better views.

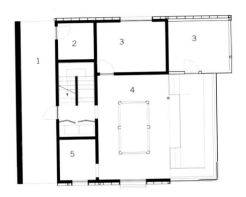

First floor

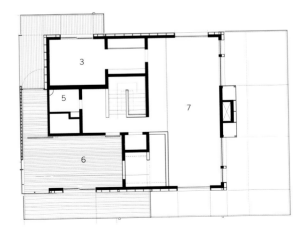

Third floor

1. Workshop
2. Storage space
3. Bedroom
4. Game room
5. Bathroom
6. Main bedroom
7. Open space

Outdoor terraces with glass panels, but with no other elements to spoil the view, were built around the house to create quiet vantage points where the owners can enjoy the landscape to the maximum.

Glass blocks were placed on the front façade; these were provided by the owner and were one of the project requirements. In addition, wooden slats serve as screens to protect the house from the rain.

The glass blocks and the many windows enable
the light to enter all rooms in the house. The house
also has a rainwater collection system to collect
water for the swimming pools and water tanks.

J2 House

Architect: 3LHD Architects
Location: Zagreb, Croatia
Photos: © Damir Fabijanic

This project involved the renovation of an old building on a lot surrounded by streets and high buildings; these were the main aspects taken into consideration when redesigning the house.

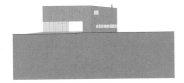

Northeast elevation

Northwest elevation

Southeast elevation

Southwest elevation

The floor was designed in an L shape and the façade has hardly any windows to provide privacy from neighbors and passersby. In addition, the main rooms look onto the garden.

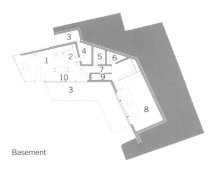

Basement

First floor

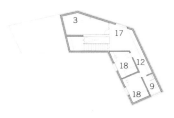

Second floor

1. Living room
2. Kitchen
3. Terrace
4. Storage space
5. Laundry room
6. Sauna
7. Stairs
8. Swimming pool
9. Bathroom
10. Dining room
11. Gallery
12. Closet
13. Guest bedroom
14. Indoor garage
15. Garage
16. Main bedroom
17. Lounge
18. Bedroom

The materials used in the façade were chosen according to the layout of the house. The public areas, for instance, have glass walls and the bedrooms have wooden panels.

Ryan Residence

Architect: Lundberg Design
Location: Larkspur, California, USA
Photos: © Art Gray, Michelle Kriebel,
Ryan Hughes

Steel and glass were mainly used in the entrance
to this home, which is a renovation of an austere
house that was built on difficult terrain.

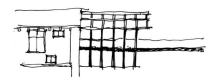

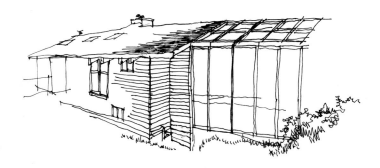

Elevation sketch

The glass and steel structure comprises the first entrance to the building and represents a sharp contrast to the poor original construction.

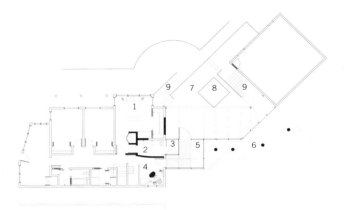

First floor (new building)

1. Bedroom
2. Bathroom
3. Shower
4. Office
5. Ecological house
6. New gateway
7. New terrace
8. Jacuzzi
9. Stairs

Second floor (new building)

1. Concrete gateway
2. Entrance to the ecological house
3. Closet and guest bathroom
4. Fireplace
5. Dining room
6. Terrace
7. Kitchen
8. Renovated terrace

The glass gateway leads to the new terraces, which were built on both floors of the building. Steel and glass were also used in the interior.

The furniture in the kitchen and the dining room table were designed and made by the architects. In the interior, the warm wood contrasts with vibrant colors like red and apple green.

Beach Lane Residence

Architect: Stelle Architects
Location: Wainscott, New York, USA
Photos: © Jeff Heatley

The main objective of this project was to modernize a 19th-century farmhouse. The original building was dismantled to the shell and then rebuilt with new foundations.

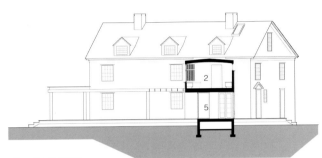

North-south section (gateway)

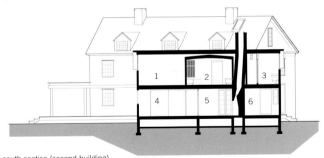

North-south section (second building)

1. Bedroom
2. Playroom
3. Bathroom
4. Kitchen
5. Gateway
6. Laundry room

A kitchen and fireplace were added and more open
and simple rooms were designed. The stairwell
connects the three levels and bathes the interior in
natural light.

The extension includes a children's bedroom, bathroom and playroom. The architects aimed to highlight the modern design of the house, while maintaining its original essence, especially on the outside.

First floor

Second floor

1. Existing building
2. Gateway
3. Kitchen
4. Laundry room
5. Entrance
6. South terrace
7. Porch
8. Existing building
9. Corridor
10. Game room
11. Bathroom
12. Bedroom

The materials used in the interior, i.e., maple wood, limestone, plaster and glass, are natural and durable. The windows and doors are of painted anodized aluminum.

Cutting Edge Houses

C House

Architect: Studio Damilano
Location: Cuneo, Milano, Italy
Photos: © Andrea Martiradonna

This house is built on a lot beside a river park.
It was built for a family of four, but is large enough
to host relatives visiting from abroad.

First floor

Basement

1. Kitchen/dining room
2. Living room
3. Suite
4. Bedroom
5. Bathroom
6. Relaxation area
7. Guest bathroom
8. Guest bedroom

The main objective of the project was to open the rooms as much as possible to create more space and to establish a dialogue between the surroundings and the house, which also has a garden.

The house has two stories: one on the ground level
and the other at semi-basement level. The
bedrooms are located on either end of the first
floor; the kitchen is also at one end, while the living
room occupies the central area connecting the
two ends.

The semi-basement level contains a small apartment to accommodate visiting relatives in a comfortable and private environment. It also has a studio and relaxation area.

Skyline Residence

Architect: Belzberg Architects
Location: Los Angeles, California, USA
Photos: © Benny Chan/Fotoworks

The most eye-catching feature of this spectacular residence is the projection screen on one of the walls of the guest house, which is perfectly visible from the main building.

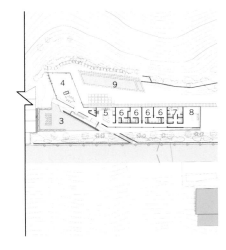

Floor plan

1. Two-story guest house
2. Seats for the outdoor movie theatre
3. Outdoor terrace with views and garage on the lower floor
4. Living/dining room
5. Kitchen
6. Guest bedroom
7. Main bathroom
8. Main bedroom
9. Swimming pool

Located in the Hollywood Hills, this home has magnificent views of Los Angeles and the adjacent hills, which was why part of the perimeter walls were replaced with glass.

One of the objectives of the project was to use sustainable materials without going over budget. The house is therefore oriented to make the most of the natural light and the materials were from the grounds itself.

The house is comprised of two structures; an
L-shaped one and the guest house and garage.
At the shorter end of the main building is the living
room, surrounded by glass, and the rest of the
rooms are at the other end of the house.

Openhouse

Architect: XTEN Architecture
Location: Hollywood Hills, California, USA
Photos: © Art Gray

This house was built on a sharp and narrow slope in the Hollywood Hills. It was a challenging project that was integrated into the landscape and faces the city of Los Angeles.

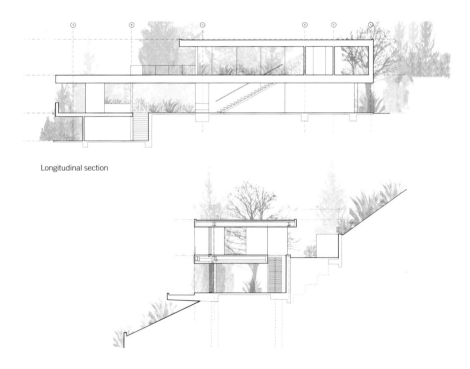

Longitudinal section

Transverse section

The retaining walls were designed to extend the first floor into the hillside, thus "stealing" space from the hill and enabling the creation of a garden terrace on the third floor.

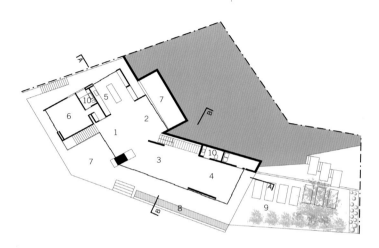

First floor

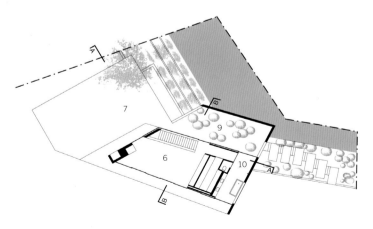

Second floor

1. Living room
2. Dining room
3. Studio
4. Game room
5. Kitchen
6. Bedroom
7. Terrace
8. Swimming pool
9. Garden
10. Bathroom

The house is almost completely open to the exterior; the front and rear façades are made entirely of glass. Glass was also used in the side walls of the first floor and on one side of the upper floor.

Glass was the main material used for the walls.
Forty-four sliding glass windows were used in total.
These become invisible when opened, thus
establishing a direct link between the interior
and exterior.

O House

Architect: Sou Fujimoto Architects
Location: Chiba, Japan
Photos: © Daici Ano

This spectacular residence is located on a rocky coast overlooking the Pacific Ocean. The front façade has large glass windows that reflect the water, while the rear of the house is made of concrete and has no windows or doors.

1. Closet
2. Tatami room
3. Kitchen
4. Dining room
5. Guest bathroom
6. Porch
7. Bedroom
8. Toilet
9. Bathroom
10. Studio
11. Living room
12. Garage

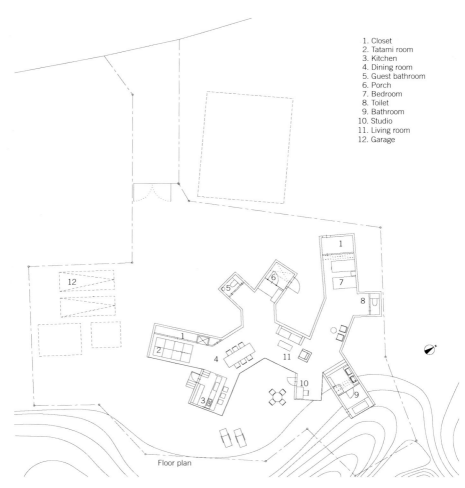

Floor plan

The house is open-plan, i.e., comprised of a single and open space shaped like the branches of a tree. Partitions are therefore avoided and almost the entire house has spectacular views.

House in Minami-Boso

Architect: Kiyonobu Nakagame & Associates
Location: Chiba, Japan
Photos: K.Torimura, N. Meguro

This house is located in Boso Peninsula to the east of Tokyo; it overlooks the Pacific Ocean and has mountains at the rear. Because of the magnificent setting, it was decided to ensure that the house had plenty of views.

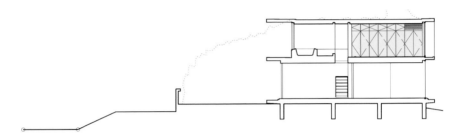

Transverse section

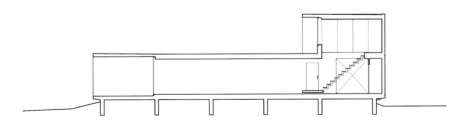

Longitudinal section

The main idea behind this project was to construct a large continuous wall that opens out in different directions, ensuring that most rooms have views. The other walls were replaced with glass.

1. Terrace
2. Hall
3. Living room
4. Dining room
5. Kitchen
6. Guest bathroom
7. Guest bedroom
8. Bedroom
9. Bathroom
10. Closet
11. Roof

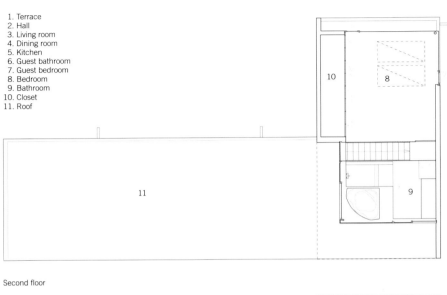

Second floor

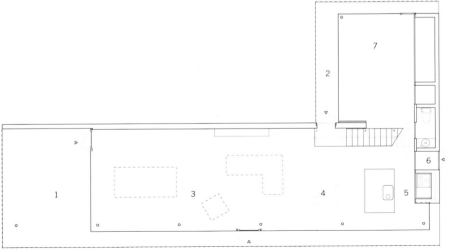

First floor

The public areas are laid out in an open-plan style on the first floor. On the same level, and on the other side of the stairs, is the guest bedroom. The porch is a magnificent corner in which to relax and enjoy the landscape.

On the upper floor, and occupying a much smaller area than the first floor, are the main bedroom and a large bathroom with a jacuzzi, with privileged views of the ocean.

Bishop Street Residence

Architect: Taylor Smyth Architects
Location: Toronto, Canada
Photos: © Ben Rahn/A-Frame

Clad in black zinc slats arranged vertically and
horizontally, the façade rises out of a concrete base
and is spattered with anodized aluminum windows.

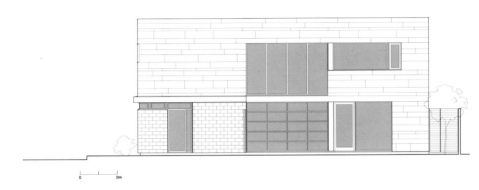

Front elevation

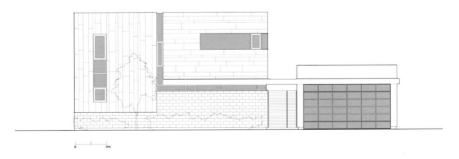

Side elevation

The sturdiness of the building exterior contrasts sharply with the compact and transparent light box in the interior, where the use of glass predominates. The garage-style door separating the living room and outdoor patio is also made of glass.

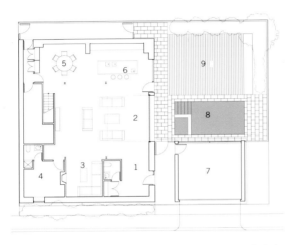

First floor

0 — 2m

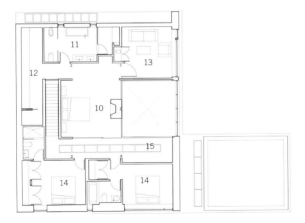

Second floor

1. Entrance
2. Living room
3. Small room
4. Laundry room
5. Dining room
6. Kitchen
7. Garage
8. Swimming pool

9. Terrace
10. Main suite
11. Suite
12. Walk-in closet
13. Studio
14. Bedroom
15. Gallery

The house was decorated with designer furniture and works of art belonging to the owner, who also collects cars. These can be admired through the glass wall of the garage.

Ravine Residence

Architect: Cindy Rendely Architexture
Location: Toronto, Canada
Photos: © Tom Arban

Located on a steep slope in Toronto, this house was designed to accommodate several generations of one family, in addition to the chauffeur and his wife.

1. Jacuzzi and sauna
2. Bathroom
3. Laundry room
4. Engine room
5. Storage space
6. Bedroom
7. Living room
8. Game room
9. Exercise room

Basement

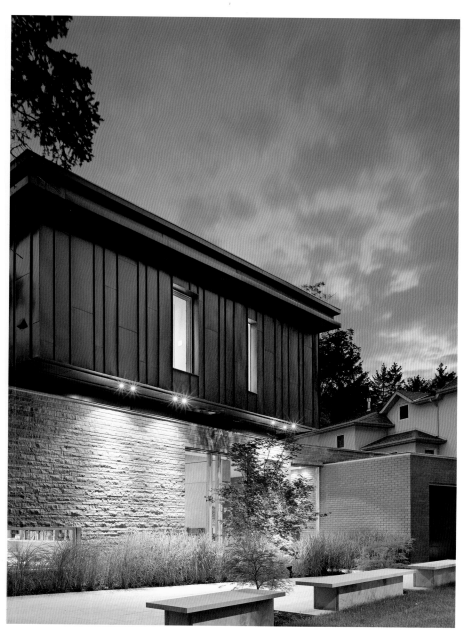

The layout is U-shaped with a patio in the center which serves as an outdoor dining room. Because of the steep terrain, the house was built on the slope and the basement opens to the exterior at one side.

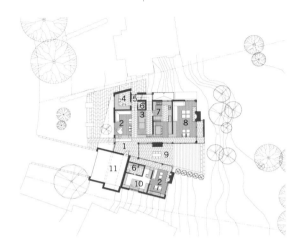

First floor

1. Entrance
2. Living room
3. Dining room
4. Studio
5. Hall
6. Bathroom
7. Kitchen
8. Lounge
9. Outdoor terrace
10. Bedroom
11. Garage
12. Laundry room
13. Storage space
14. Walk-in closet
15. Main bedroom

Second floor

The wing made of metal and stone contains the living quarters of the five family members and the servants. Across from the hall, a single-story building houses the garage and a small apartment for the grandparents.

Cohen-Collins Residence

Architect: Michael Singer and Aaron Kadoch
Location: Northhampton, Massachusetts, USA
Photos: © David Stansbury

This 5,005 sq. ft. home is a marriage of steel and wood. It was built around a central gallery that serves as a passageway and extends from the entrance of the house to the terrace in the south.

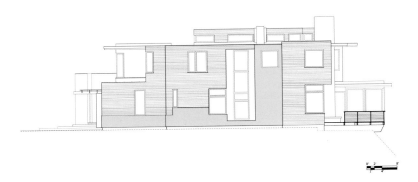

East elevation

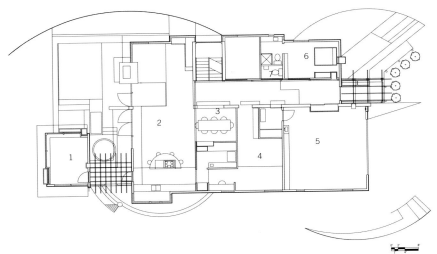

1. Small room
2. Kitchen
3. Dining room
4. Bedroom/studio
5. Living room
6. Suite
7. Bathroom

Floor plan

Located on top of a hill, the new house was built on the foundations of an earlier building, but these were modified so that the house would project over the slope.

The objectives of the project were to save energy through the use of solar and geothermal power systems, to make the most of the natural light and magnificent views, to achieve privacy, and to design a space that was conducive to family life.

Ellsworth Residence

Architect: Michael P Johnson Design Studios
Location: Cave Creek, Arizona, USA
Photos: © Bill Timmerman

This project was a difficult challenge for the
architects, as the house was to be built in
the desert of Arizona. In the end, a long building
was constructed on a curved lot.

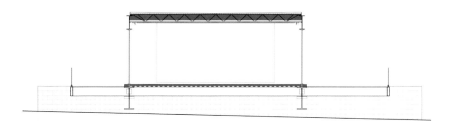

Transverse section

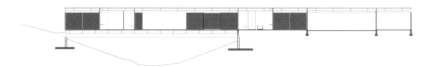

Longitudinal section

Because the house belongs to an art collector, there was the added challenge of creating a gallery to exhibit art and furniture in addition to the living quarters.

Space was reserved beside the spacious living
room and dining room to exhibit a specially
commissioned installation by the artist Mayme
Kratz. In addition, this part of the house has
extensive views of the desert.

1. Bedroom
2. Bathroom
3. Closet
4. Guest bathroom
5. Dining room
6. Kitchen
7. Balcony
8. Living room
9. Entrance gateway
10. Garage
11. Guest bathroom
12. Guest bedroom
13. Terrace

Floor plan

The house has two main bedrooms with adjoining bathrooms, a storage room, kitchen—beside the dining room—and a guest bedroom which is separated from the rest of the house by an indoor garage.

The main materials used in its construction are high-quality glass and steel. The floors were covered with Italian ceramic tiles.

Bay Residence

Architect: Stelle Architects
Location: Amagansett, New York, USA
Photos: © Jeff Heatley

A wooden walkway leads from the garage to the
first floor of the house and continues past bramble
thickets until reaching the beach. The second floor
occupies a raised glass block that has ocean views
and summer breezes.

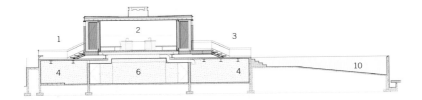

Transverse section

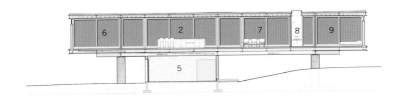

Longitudinal section

1. Entrance
2. Kitchen
3. Terrace
4. Storage space
5. Garage
6. Game room
7. Dining room
8. Guest bathroom
9. Guest bedroom
10. Swimming pool

Teak lattices break the monotony of the glass. In the south, they serve as *brise-soleils*, providing shade from the sun and privacy for the interior.

The stairs leading to the public areas are hidden
behind a wooden lattice. The interior décor was
kept simple in order to give prominence to
the landscape, which becomes yet another
decorative element.

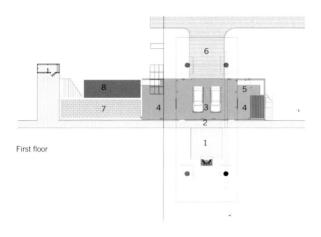

First floor

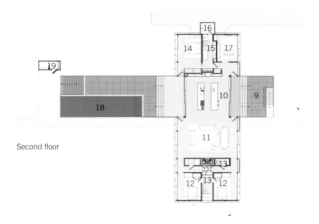

Second floor

1. Outdoor fireplace
2. Walkway
3. Garage
4. Storage space
5. Engine room
6. Gravel path
7. Swimming pool foundation
8. Swimming pool machinery
   and storage space
9. Entrance patio
10. Kitchen
11. Living room
12. Guest bedroom
13. Bathroom
14. Main bedroom
15. Main bathroom
16. Outdoor shower
17. Game room
18. Swimming pool
19. Outdoor shower

The two islands situated in the center of the kitchen stand out. The main bedroom is located in the east side of the house, while the guest bedrooms are on the west.

House at Chauncey Close

Architect: Leroy Street Studio Architecture
Location: East Hampton, Long Island,
New York, USA
Photos: © Adrian Wilson

This house has all the advantages of a traditional
barn, such as space and simplicity, but with
modern touches. One of the requirements was to
preserve the privacy of the family.

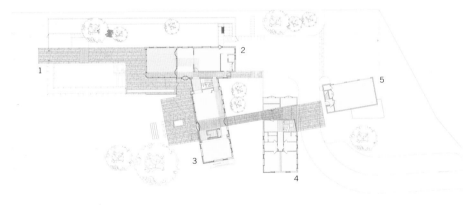

Location map

1. Swimming pool house
2. Main suite
3. Public rooms
4. Children's rooms
5. Garage/gym

Wooden panels protect the house from the rain, while unifying the interior and exterior and creating a simple volume.

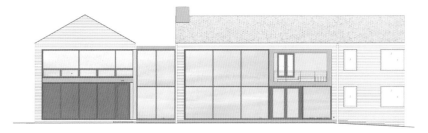

West elevation

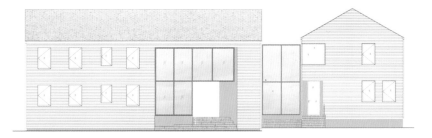

East elevation

The main door is located in a wooden façade leading to a three-story glass area that divides the building.

The public areas are located on the second floor, which has magnificent views of the ocean. There is a window at the top of the wall.

The studio, terrace, living room (with a double-height ceiling) and porch open onto each other, blurring the boundary between the interior and exterior.

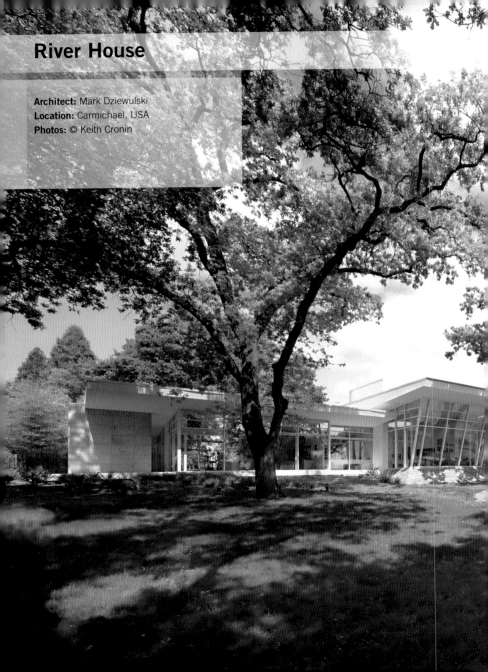

River House

Architect: Mark Dziewulski
Location: Carmichael, USA
Photos: © Keith Cronin

Located on a gentle forest slope with views across the river and to the park on the opposite bank, this house seems to be sculpted by the natural setting that surrounds it. The old trees provide shade and natural protection.

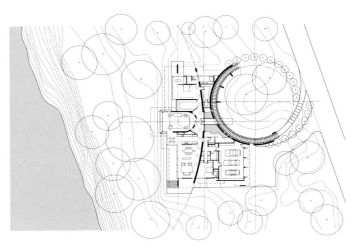

Site Plan

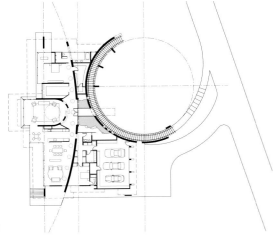

Floor plan

The design of the home includes service spaces and a garage on one hand, an living and relaxation areas on the other. The whole of the house opens onto the living room, a long continuous space.

Mimetic House

Architect: Dominic Stevens
Location: Dromahair, County Leitrim, Ireland
Photos: © Ros Kavanagh

This house, built in the middle of green fields and meadows, defies classical categorization and dwells on the boundaries of standard perception. It consists of an underground part and an above-ground, glass-encased multipurpose room.

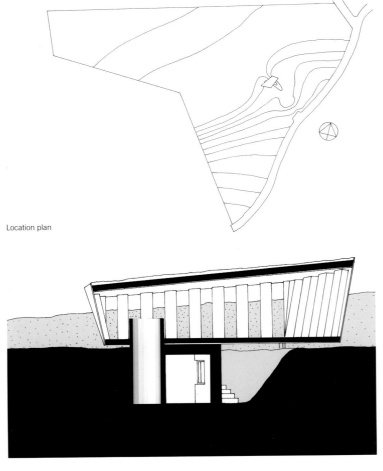

Location plan

Section

Owing the use of semireflective glass, the building appears entirely transparent or it reflects the surrounding landscape, making impossible to see in.

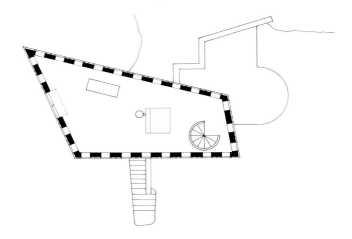

Second floor

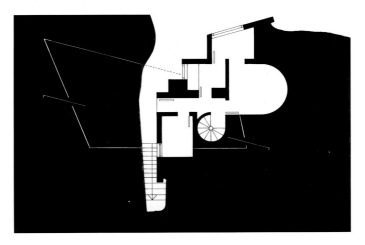

First floor

The façade consists of vertical glass strips, some transparent, some reflective. When it is dark, the house becomes a minimalistic light-sculpture.

House in Las Arenas

Architect: Artadi Arquitectos
Location: Lima, Peru
Photos: © Alexander Kornhuber

The freight container was the starting point of the design of this beach house 62 miles south of Lima. By raising the boxlike main section over the base the building appears to float above the ground.

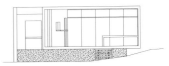

West façade

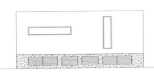

East façade

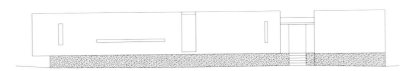

South façade

To limit the amount of sunlight that enters the
rooms several slots were added to the construction.
A terrace, with a long bench and massive table,
overlooking the sea is the most important feature of
this minimalist house.

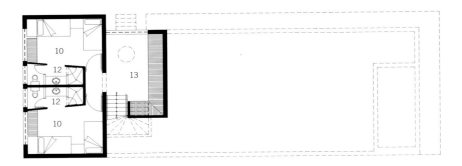

Basement

First floor

1. Entryway
2. Lounge
3. Dining room
4. Terrace
5. Pool
6. Kitchen
7. Powder room
8. Storage
9. Laundry room
10. Bedrooms
11. Master bedroom
12. Bathrooms
13. TV room

By using simple materials a powerful impression can be created: precise slots in the outer volume provide an unobstructed view of the horizon. A straight path leads directly from the outdoor relaxation area to the beach.

Avenel House

Architect: Paul Morgan Architects
Location: Central Victoria, Australia
Photos: © Gollings Photography

The design of this four-bedroom house, situated on an extensive terrain in a rural area of Central Victoria –a region known for its intense sun and strong winds– was inspired by the dynamic landscape elements apparent at this exposed countryside setting.

North-South Section

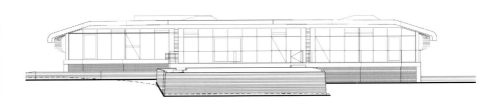

Elevation

The ecological conditions of the site were used to generate formal and spatial qualities in the design. Enormous glass surfaces ensure the landscape can be enjoyed from within while the roof protects interiors from harsh light.

This house combines a lightweight metal skin with a grounded stone and concrete base. Horizontal wooden slats shade the windows on the narrow side of the house. The main materials used throughout the construction are concrete and blue-gray granite.

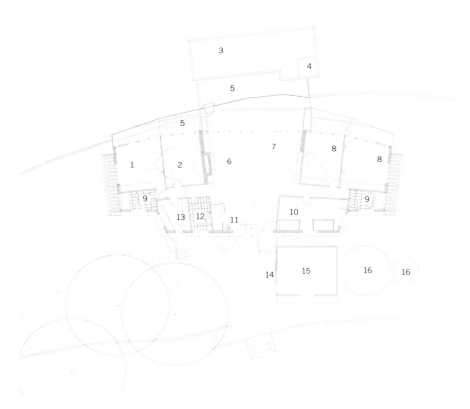

Floor plan

1. Master bedroom
2. Study
3. Pool
4. Spa
5. Terrace
6. Lounge
7. Dining room
8. Bedrooms
9. Ensuites
10. Play room
11. Kicthen
12. Bathrooms
13. Laudry room
14. Courtyard
15. Shed
16. Water tank

3LHD Architects
Božidarevića 13/4
Zagreb 10000, Croatia
P. +385 1 232 0200
info@3lhd.com
www.3lhd.com

Acn+Architektur
Schopenhauerstrasse 19/2/15
1180 Vienna, Austria
P. +43 1 968 27 63
office@acnplus.at

Adrián Moreno, María Samaniego/Arquitectura X
Av. Granda Centeno 1114 y Bobadilla 16
Quito, Ecuador
P. +593 2 227 8772
amoreno@arquitecturax.com
www.arquitecturax.com

Aidlin Darling Design
500 Third Street, Suite 410
San Francisco, CA 94107, USA
P. +1 415 974 5603
info@aidlindarlingdesign.com
www.aidlindarlingdesign.com

Aleš Vodopivec
Kladezna 14
1000 Ljubljana, Slovenia
P. +386 1 251 12 36
ales.vodopivec@fa.uni-lj.si

Álvaro Ramírez and Clarisa Elton
El rey 0706 Providencia
7530018 Santiago de Chile, Chile
P. +562 953 5248
alvaro@ramirez-moletto.cl
www.ramirez-moletto.cl

Artadi Arquitectos
Camino Real 111 Of. 701 San Isidro
Lima, Peru
P. +51 1 222 6261
artadi@speedy.com.pe
www.javierartadi.com

Atelier Oï
Ch. du Signolet 3
2520 La Neuveville, Switzerland
P. +41 32 751 56 66
contact@atelier-oi.ch
www.atelier-oi.ch

Belzberg Architects
1501 Colorado Ave., Suite B
Santa Monica, CA 90404, USA
P. +1 310 453 9611
studio@belzbergarchitects.com
www.belzbergarchitects.com

Bercy Chen Studio LLP
1111 E. 11th Street Studio 200
Austin, TX 78702, USA
P. +1 512 481 0092
info@bcarc.com
www.bcarc.com

Blank Studio
1441 East Sunnyside Drive
Phoenix, AZ 85020, USA
P. +1 602 331 3310
studio@blankspaces.net
www.blankspaces.net

BURO II bvba
Hoogleedsesteenweg 415
8800 Roeselare, Belgium
T +32 51 21 11 05
info@buro2.be
www.buro2.be, www.buro-interior.be

Cary Bernstein
2325 Third St. Studio 341
San Francisco, CA 94107, USA
P. +1 415 522 1907
cary@cbstudio.com
www.cbstudio.com

Cindy Rendely Architexture
5 Sultan Street N° 202
Toronto M5S 1L6, Canada
P. +1 416 924 9696
cindy@crarchitexture.com
www.crarchitexture.com

Darren Petrucci
8604 E. Via de los Libros
Scottsdale, AZ 85258, USA
P. +1 480 329 1888
darren.petrucci@asu.edu

Dominic Stevens Architect
www.dominicstevensarchitect.net

Eduardo Cadaval & Clara Solà-Morales
Avenir 1, ppal 1a
08006 Barcelona, Spain
P. +34 93 414 37 14
studio@ca-so.com
www.ca-so.com

Emma Doherty & Amanda Menage
76 Bermondsey Street
London SE1 3UD, UK
P. +44 7961 123 074
amanda@bstreetstudio.co.uk
www.bstreetstudio.co.uk

Eric Haesloop, Mary Griffin/Turnbull Griffin Haesloop Architects
1660 Bush St. Suite 200
San Francisco, CA 94109, USA
P. +1 415 441 2300
info@tgharchitects.com
www.tgharchitects.com

Exe Arquitectura
Bolivia 340, local 64C
08019 Barcelona, Spain
P. +34 93 200 80 35
info@exearquitectura.com
www.exearquitectura.com

Felipe Assadi & Francisca Pulido
Malaga 940, Las Condes
Santiago, Chile
P. + 562 263 57 38
info@assadi.cl
www.assadi.cl

GAD Architecture
29 Broadway, Suite 1707
New York, NY 10006, USA
P. +1 917 338 1395
gadny@gadarchitecture.com
www.gadarchitecture.com

GRID Architekten
Hammer-Purgstallgasse 5-4
1020 Vienna, Austria
P. +43 1 925 31 96
mail@thegrids.net
www.thegrids.net

Hiromasa Mori & Takuya Hosokai/1980
Hiromasa Mori
hhiim@yahoo.co.jp
Takuya Hosokai
01@takuyahosokai.com

Ibarra Rosano Design Architects
2849 East Sylvia Street
Tucson, AZ 85716, USA
P. +1 520 795 5477
mail@ibarrarosano.com
www.ibarrarosano.com

Jarmund/Vigsnæs AS Architects MNAL
Hausmanns Gate 6
0186 Oslo, Norway
P. +47 22 99 43 43
jva@jva.no
www.jva.no

Jeff Brock and Belén Moneo/Moneo Brock Studio
Fco Asís Méndez Casariego 7
28002 Madrid, Spain
P. +91 563 80 56
contact@moneobrock.com
www.moneobrock.com

John Friedman and Alice Kimm Architects
701 East Third Street, Suite 300
Los Angeles, CA 90013-1843, USA
P. +1 213 253 4740
jfak@jfak.net
www.jfak.net

Juan Carlos Doblado
Miguel Dasso 139
Of. 702 San Isidro, Perú
P. +51 421 3857
info@juancarlosdoblado.com
www.juancarlosdoblado.com

Kimmo Friman/friman.laaksonen arkkitehdit Oy
Töölöntorinkatu 2 B 9. krs
0026 Helsinki, Finland
P. +358 505 11 4447
Kimmo.friman@fl-a.fi
www.fl-a.fi

Kiyonobu Nakagame & Associates
1-11-1 B1 Shishigaya Tsurumi-ku
Yokohama City, Kanagawa 230-0073, Japan
Tel. +81 45 581 9812
info@nakagame.com
www.nakagame.com

Landau & Kindelbacher Architekten – Innerarchitekten
Thierschstrasse 17
80538 München, Germany
P. +1 49 89 242289
info@landaukindelbacher.de
www.landaukindelbacher.de

Lundberg Design
2620 Thrid Street
San Francisco, CA 94107, USA
P. +1 415 695 0110
info@lundbergdesign.com
www.lundbergdesign.com

Mark Dziewulski
500 Third Street, Suite 210
San Francisco, Califonia 94107, USA
P. +1 415 882 7808
office@DZarchitect.com
www.dzarchitect.com

Martin Schneider Architektur
Ubierring 47
50678 Köln, Germany
P. +49 221 932 18 79
ms@ms-arc.de
www.ms-arc.de

Michael Meredith, Hilary Sample/MOS
92 William Street
New Haven, CT 06511, USA
P. +1 646 797 3046
info@mos-office.net
www.mos-office.net

Michael P Johnson Design Studios Ltd.
P.O. Box 4058
Cave Creek, AZ 85327, USA
P. +1 480 488 2691
michael@mpjstudio.com
www.mpjstudio.com

Michael Singer y Aaron Kadoch
msinger@sover.net
www.michaelsinger.com

Min I Day
2325 Third Street, Studio 425
San Francisco, 94107, USA
P. +1 415 255 9464
info@minday.com
www.minday.com

MVRDV bv
Dunantstraat 10
3024 BC Rotterdam, The Netherlands
P. +31 10 477 28 60
office@mvrdv.nl
www.mvrdv.nl

Neil M. Denari Architects
12615 Washington Boulevard
Los Angeles, CA 90066, USA
P. +1 310 390 3033
info@nmda-inc.com
www.nmda-inc.com

Nicholas Murray Architects
7 Hotham Street, South Melbourne
Victoria 3205, Australia
P. +61 9686 0718
nicholas@nma.net.au
www.nma.net.a

Nobbs Radford Architects
Level 1, 16 Foster Street
Surry Hills NSW 2010, Australia
P. + 61 2 9281 2722
architects@nobbsradford.com.au
www.nobbsradford.com.au

Olavi Koponen
Apollonkatu 23 B 39
Helsinki, Finland
P. +358 9 44 10 96
olavi.koponen@kolumbus.fi
www.kolumbus.fi/olavi.koponen/

Paul Cha
611 Broadway, Suite 540
New York, NY 10012, USA
P. +1 212 477 6957
mail@paulchaarchitectcom
www.paulchaarchitect.com

Paul Morgan Architects
Level 10, 221 Queen Street
3000 Melbourne, Victoria, Australia
P. +61 3 9650 4100
office@paulmorganarchitects.com
www.paulmorganarchitects.com

Pezo von Ellrichshausen Architects
Lo Pequén 502
Concepción, Chile
P. +56 41 221 0281
info@pezo.cl
www.pezo.cl

Ronan & Erwan Bouroullec
23, rue du Buisson Saint-Louis
75010 Paris, France
info@bouroullec.com
www.bouroullec.com

SHA Scheffler Helbich Architekten GmbH
Schwerter Straße 264
44287 Dortmund, Germany
P. +49 231 44 20200
info@scheffler-helbich.de
www.scheffler-helbich.de

Sou Fujimoto Architects
164-0013 Tokyo-to Nakano-ku Yayoi-chou
2-7-5 Meitoh-K Bldg B1F, Japan
P. +81 35 351 8136
www.sou-fujimoto.com

SPF:a
8609 E. Washington Boulevard
Culver City, CA 90232, USA
P. +1 310 558 0902
dafna@spfa.com
www.spfa.com

SPG Architects
127 West 26th Street 800
New York, NY 10001, USA
P. +1 212 366 5500
contact@spgarchitects.com
www.spgarchitects.com

Stelle Architects
48 Foster Avenue, PO Box 3002
Bridgehampton, NY 11932, USA
P. +1 631 537 0019
info@stelleco.com
www.stelleco.com

Studio 804
1465 Jayhawk Blvd., Marvin Hall Rm 105
Lawrence, KS, 66045-0001, USA
P. +1 785 393 0747
rockhill@ku.edu, rockhill@sunflower.com
www.studio804.com

Studio Damilano
Via Vecchia di Cuneo 128
12011 Borgo San Dalmazzo, Italy
P. +39 171 262 924
d.damilano@gmail.com
www.damilanostudio.com

Studio Giovanni D'Ambrosio
Via Monserrato, 34
00186 Rome, Italy
P. +39 06 6869760
www.giovannidambrosio.com

Takaharu & Yui Tezuka/Tezuka Architects
Masahiro Ikeda/Masahiro Ikeda Co., ltd
1-19-9-3F Todoroki Setagaya
158-0082 Tokyo, Japan
P. +81 33 703 7056
tez@sepia.ocn.ne.jp
www.tezuka-arch.com

Taylor Smyth Architects
354 Davenport Road, Suite 3B
Toronto, Ontario M5R 1K6, Canada
P. +1 416 968 6688
info@taylorsmyth.com
www.taylorsmyth.com

Teeple Architects
5 Camden Street
Toronto, Ontario M5V 1V2, Canada
P. +1 416 598 0554
info@teeplearch.com
www.teeplearch.com

Tomoko Anyoji & Yannick Beltrando Architects
322 rue des Pyrénées
75020 Paris, France
P. +33 1 42 71 01 28
Tomoko.anyoji@orange.fr

UCArchitect
283 Lisgar Street
Toronto, Ontario M6J 3H1, Canada
P. +1 416 536 4977
phe@ucarchitect.ca
www.ucarchitect.ca

XTEN Architecture
201 South Santa Fe Ave., Suite 202
Los Angeles, CA 90012, USA
P. +1 213 625 7002
info@xtenarchitecture.com
www.xtenarchitecture.com

Yasuhiro Yamashita and Yoichi Tanaka/ Atelier Tekuto
301-6-15-16 Honkomagome, Bunkyo-ku
113-0021 Tokyo, Japan
P. +81 3 5940 2770
info@tekuto.com
www.tekuto.com